OVERCOMING
FAMILIAR
SPIRITS

OVERCOMING

FAMILIAR

SPIRITS

DELIVERANCE FROM **UNSEEN DEMONIC ENEMIES** AND **SPIRITUAL DEBT**

KYNAN BRIDGES

WHITAKER
HOUSE

Unless otherwise indicated, all Scripture quotations are taken from the *King James Easy Read Bible*, KJVER®, © 2001, 2007, 2010, 2015 by Whitaker House. Used by permission. All rights reserved. Scripture quotations marked (RSV) are taken from the *Revised Standard Version of the Bible*, © 1946, 1952, 1971 by the Division of Christian Education of the National Council of Churches of Christ in the U.S.A. Used by permission. All rights reserved. Scripture quotations marked (NLT) are taken from the *Holy Bible, New Living Translation*, © 1996, 2004, 2015 by Tyndale House Foundation. Used by permission of Tyndale House Publishers, Inc., Carol Stream, Illinois 60188. All rights reserved. Scripture quotations marked (NKJV) are taken from the *New King James Version*, © 1979, 1980, 1982 by Thomas Nelson, Inc. Used by permission. All rights reserved.

Boldface type in the Scripture quotations indicates the author's emphasis. The forms LORD and GOD (in small capital letters) in Bible quotations represent the Hebrew name for God *Yahweh* (Jehovah), while *Lord* and *God* normally represent the name *Adonai*, in accordance with the Bible version used.

Some definitions of Greek words are taken from the New Testament Greek Lexicon—King James Version or New American Standard, based on Thayer's and Smith's Bible Dictionary, plus others (public domain), www.BibleStudyTools.com. Some definitions of Hebrew words are taken from the Old Testament Hebrew Lexicon—King James Version or New American Standard, which is the Brown, Driver, Briggs, Gesenius Lexicon (public domain), BibleStudyTools.com. Other Greek and Hebrew definitions are taken from the resources of blueletterBible.org and the electronic version of *Strong's Exhaustive Concordance of the Bible*, STRONG (© 1980, 1986, and assigned to World Bible Publishers, Inc. Used by permission. All rights reserved.).

OVERCOMING FAMILIAR SPIRITS:
Deliverance from Unseen Demonic Enemies and Spiritual Debt

Kynan Bridges Ministries, Inc.
P.O. Box 159 • Ruskin, FL 33575
www.kynanbridges.com
info@kynanbridges.com

ISBN: 978-1-64123-797-0 • eBook ISBN: 978-1-64123-798-7
Printed in the United States of America
© 2022 by Kynan Bridges

Whitaker House
1030 Hunt Valley Circle • New Kensington, PA 15068
www.whitakerhouse.com

Library of Congress Control Number: 2022931479

3 4 5 6 7 8 9 10 11 ⊞ 29 28 27 26 25 24 23

CONTENTS

PREFACE

Overcoming *Familiar Spirits: Deliverance from Unseen Demonic Enemies and Spiritual Debt* has been one of the most challenging books I have ever written—and it may be the most controversial. In this book, I discuss the shocking truth about demonic entities called *familiar spirits*. I specifically deal with how we can become free of familiar spirits by understanding spiritual debt, breaking unhealthy soul ties and agreements, and releasing demonic liens.

You likely know something about evil spirits and unhealthy soul ties, but you may be unfamiliar with the term *demonic liens*. In the natural world, a lien is a legal hold or claim against someone's property until a debt is paid. The Lord has shown me that many believers are trapped by spiritual debt and ensnared by demonic liens, and this is why they are continually being hindered in their lives and unable to fulfill God's purposes for them. They are being oppressed in their marriages, their finances, their ministries, and other areas.

The purpose of this book is to finally identify the culprit of so many common and constant struggles that believers, out of ignorance of spiritual truths, have conformed to, thus giving the enemy access. When people have had their minds and bodies bombarded by familiar spirits, they often feel discouraged and beyond hope. They think God disapproves of them and can never use them. Yet the Lord God Jehovah loves us and wants to break the demonic liens in our lives so we can experience freedom and abundant life. God desires that we confront these demonic forces and reestablish our place of spiritual authority in any areas where familiar spirits have taken residence. He wants us to exercise dominion on the earth and have victory over the enemy's schemes.

Now understand this: I speak from personal experience. There were things in my life that were giving the devil legal access to me, and I did not even realize it. At the beginning, I was not even aware that familiar spirits existed or how to combat them, and that is why the same demons kept showing up through different people and circumstances, time and time again, with the same temptations, the same difficulties, the same obstacles, the same troubling dreams, the same issues, over and over again.

When I began to understand the nature of familiar spirits, I still needed additional revelation and insight. While I was consulting the Lord concerning this topic, I asked Him why certain things in my own life continued to perpetually afflict me. I am filled with the Holy Spirit, I am anointed by the Spirit, and I pray in tongues. So, why were there areas where oppression seemed to be continually present and particular sins were a recurring problem? The revelation of deliverance that I received and that I present in this book has been life-changing not only for me but for many other believers with whom I have shared these truths.

Even writing this book required much soul-searching and repentance on my part so that I could clearly articulate, from a pure and sincere place, God's heart of love to give us the freedom and deliverance we need. Through this process, I was able to identify places in my mind and emotions that required deeper levels of healing and deliverance, and God gave me the grace to overcome in these areas. My prayer is that you will be impacted by the liberating presence and power of God in the same way. I also pray that you will come to receive the revelation that the source of our freedom begins and ends in Jesus Christ and the Word of God.

In *Overcoming Familiar Spirits*, I discuss both my experiences and others' experiences in dealing with familiar spirits, and what the access points of so many of these demonic entities are. I also show the scriptural basis for how we can take back our spiritual authority over the enemy. In these pages, you will find real-life stories, anecdotes, and biblical examples to help you discern and have victory over familiar spirits.

God is saying that it is time for us to be released from all spiritual debt. It is time to be set free from all demonic liens on our bloodlines, our minds, our emotions, our bodies, our finances, our marriages, our other relationships, and our destinies, in Jesus's name! As you discover how to receive this freedom and put into practice *Overcoming Familiar Spirits*, may your life never be the same again.

1

UNWANTED GUESTS

"For we wrestle not against flesh and blood, but against principalities, against powers, against the rulers of the darkness of this world, against spiritual wickedness in high places."
—Ephesians 6:12

People all over the world—including many dedicated Christians—are struggling in cyclical patterns of defeat. They are silently crying out, "Why do I keep going through this issue time and time again?" They spend a large portion of their lives struggling with various sins, difficulties, and types of spiritual bondage. It might be continual conflict in their marriage, a prolonged inability to conceive, incessant financial difficulties, a sense of being mired in the past, or any one of a number of other issues. They constantly live with frustration, worry, anger, or a sense of hopelessness, thinking there is no way out. They may even feel that some type of evil manifestation is oppressing them.

Over the years, as a pastor, teacher, and counselor, I have come across many such individuals, and their burdens have become my burden. I began to ask the Lord why these cyclical patterns were occurring, and He faithfully shared answers with me as I grew spiritually in my own personal experiences, studied God's Word, and ministered to His people.

Through all my questions and seeking, I came to the realization that millions of people are being tormented by demonic powers called "familiar spirits" that hide behind the mental and emotional framework of their victims. These spirits operate inconspicuously within the fabric of people's mindsets, thoughts, and emotions to a degree that they are undetected by their "hosts."

In my book *Kingdom Authority*, I shared a story I heard about a family who bought a house in the suburbs. After living there for several years, they made a shocking discovery. The two sons of the family were playing, and one of the brothers accidentally bumped against a built-in bookcase, which opened to reveal a secret passageway that led to a spiral staircase. The young men got a flashlight and went down the stairs to investigate. To their surprise, they found a living space within the walls of the house. There were cups, napkins, and utensils that seemed to have been recently used. This discovery was absolutely terrifying for the boys. Unbeknownst to them, people had been living in the family home out of sight as they and their parents had gone about their daily lives. Can you imagine finding out that strangers have been living in your home without your knowledge?

I don't know whether this is a true story, but it serves as a perfect illustration of the insidious nature of familiar spirits. Just like the secret guests who were living within the walls of the family home, familiar spirits occupy "rooms" in people's lives, usually without their conscious consent. In coming chapters, I will describe in more detail how this process occurs. These spirits cause people to have diminished spiritual vision and prevent them from fulfilling their full destinies. Familiar spirits are frequently behind people's inability to marry, conceive children, or attain lasting success; they are also the culprits behind premature death. This book will expose the demonic agenda and nature of familiar spirits and equip you with the tools to enjoy lasting freedom in Christ.

FAMILIAR SPIRITS OPERATE INCONSPICUOUSLY WITHIN THE FABRIC OF PEOPLE'S MINDSETS, THOUGHTS, AND EMOTIONS TO A DEGREE THAT THEY ARE UNDETECTED BY THEIR "HOSTS."

WHAT ARE FAMILIAR SPIRITS?

First, what exactly are familiar spirits? When the Bible mentions someone who "consulted familiar spirits," it typically indicates a person who attempted to speak with a deceased individual, or to an evil spiritual entity that emulated or impersonated an individual who was dead:

> The term is generally used to refer to the spirit of a dead person which professed mediums claimed they could summon for consultation (Deut. 18:11). The word "familiar" has in this phrase the sense of the Latin *familiaris*, belonging to one's family, and hence ready to serve one as a servant. Such a spirit was thought to be able to reveal the future (Isa. 8:19; 1 Sam. 28:7).[1]

In the ancient world, people would often consult individuals with familiar spirits in order to commune with the dead. This ungodly practice is called *necromancy*. However, the "dead" they were communing with were not actually deceased persons but rather evil spirits or demons.

In the Old Testament, the Israelites were warned against consorting with familiar spirits and those who dealt with the realm of darkness:

> *And when they shall say to you, Seek to them that have familiar spirits, and to wizards that peep [whisper], and that mutter: should not a people seek to their God? for the living to the dead?*   (Isaiah 8:19)

> *Regard not them that have familiar spirits, neither seek after wizards, to be defiled by them: I am the LORD your God.*   (Leviticus 19:31)

Throughout the New Testament, the existence and activity of "unclean spirits" is recorded. (See, for example, Matthew 10:1; Mark 1:23–27; Luke 9:37–42.) Many of these unclean spirits are familiar spirits, too, called by a different name. It is important to understand that the name of a spirit is associated with its behavior or function. Thus, an *unclean* spirit defiles or contaminates the person it attacks, possesses, or oppresses. Whether familiar spirits enter people's lives through necromancy or other avenues

---

1. Merrill C. Tenney, gen. ed., *The Zondervan Pictorial Bible Dictionary* (Grand Rapids, MI: Regency Reference Library, 1983), 275.

that we will discuss in this book, they always have a nefarious assignment, as evidenced by the pain and havoc they produce in the lives of their victims.

WHY ARE THEY CALLED "FAMILIAR" SPIRITS?

These evil spirits are called "familiar" because they are attached to specific individuals, families, bloodlines, or places. The Bible makes reference to generational curses or generational iniquity and the presence of sinful patterns in people's lives. For example, even though David was forgiven by God for his sins of adultery and murder, a number of his children, including Amnon and Solomon, fell into sexual perversion. (See, for example, 2 Samuel 13:1–20; 1 Kings 11:1–11.)

The reason why familiar spirits have so much insight into family members, and the reason why some people struggle with the same type of affliction over and over again, is that the spirits have been assigned to that particular family line and are instructed to watch its members. A familiar spirit has an attachment to a particular area or areas of a person's life. They are acquainted with that person's mindsets and patterns of living. Unless these spirits are forced to leave by the authority and power of God, they are able to attack family bloodlines for generations.

THE ORIGIN OF UNCLEAN SPIRITS

Unclean spirits, or demons, originate from the kingdom of darkness—the kingdom of that age-old foe the devil. Scripture describes the devil as ancient. (See Revelation 20:2.) He is ancient because he has been around since before the beginning of the human race. Certain theologians and other students of the Bible believe there were fallen angels on earth before Adam and Eve were created. (See, for example, Isaiah 14:12–14; Ezekiel 28:15–19; Revelation 12:9.) Regardless of your theological position on the origin of demons and when they first arrived on earth, it is important to understand, without equivocation, that familiar spirits are demons on assignment from Satan to hinder and attack human beings. These spirits are very real—and they are very evil. Think of them as invisible entities who have a mind, a will, and emotions, and who are able to inhabit, influence, and even torment their human hosts. They are able to inflict people with sickness and disease. They are able to cause confusion, depression, and despair.

Imagine you owned a property that was in the process of being developed into apartments. Then, random vagrants moved onto that property and began to live there. Now imagine that these "tenants" begin to wreak havoc and destruction, tearing down walls, destroying equipment, and defecating on everything. You would probably do everything in your power to confront and stop such appalling, unwanted activity. This analogy perfectly describes the nature of demonic spirits: they are insidious, nefarious, and destructive vagrants looking for someone to destroy, just as their leader the devil does. (See, for example, 1 Peter 5:8.) The influence of these demonic forces must be broken. We must allow them no place in our lives! We need to learn how to recognize the enemy's evil schemes. To do so, we have to know how familiar spirits operate.

MASTERS OF DISGUISE

One of the enemy's profound weapons is darkness and secrecy. The devil loves to operate in anonymity and disguise. In fact, this is the source of his influence.

And no marvel; for Satan himself is transformed into an angel of light. (2 Corinthians 11:14)

The enemy of our souls masquerades as an angel of light. Why? Because he and his demons are more effective when they are pretending to be someone or something other than what they really are. For instance, demons try to infiltrate the belief systems of their victims. A large part of the enemy's agenda is to rail accusations against believers. (See Revelation 12:10.) And because their goal is to remain unnoticed and undetected, they mask their suggestions and promptings as the thoughts and suggestions of those they are trying to influence. If they can get people to believe that the erroneous thoughts they are thinking actually come from their own minds, then those people will be more prone to accept the false ideas. If they can convince people that what is oppressing them is actually a part of themselves or is normal, then they can keep those people in a cycle of guilt, shame, and defeat. Such a cycle leads to frustration, discouragement, and even hopelessness and despair.

The worst case of demonic oppression is when an individual is unaware that they are being demonically attacked. But what if some people realized that the depression they have been battling is rooted in demonic activity? What if a couple considering divorce knew that they were harboring a marriage-breaking spirit? What if certain people struggling with fear understood that an evil spirit was attempting to terrorize them? Such knowledge would change the way they approached the challenges in their lives; they would recognize that they were not wrestling against other human beings or themselves but against unseen powers of darkness that need to be spiritually removed.

> **IF FAMILIAR SPIRITS CAN CONVINCE PEOPLE THAT WHAT IS OPPRESSING THEM IS ACTUALLY A PART OF THEMSELVES OR IS NORMAL, THEN THEY CAN KEEP THOSE PEOPLE IN A CYCLE OF GUILT, SHAME, AND DEFEAT.**

RULERS OF THE DARKNESS

The apostle Paul wrote in Ephesians 6:12,

For we wrestle not against flesh and blood, but against principalities, against powers, against the rulers of the darkness of this world, against spiritual wickedness in high places.

Under divine inspiration, Paul used this very interesting and powerful term: *"rulers of the darkness...."* The first portion of this phrase, *"rulers,"* is translated from the Greek word *kosmokratōr*, which means "lord of the world," or "prince of this age." Jesus referred to Satan as *"the prince of this world"* (John 12:31; 14:30; 16:11).

The second part of the above phrase from Ephesians 6:12 is "*darkness*," which is translated from the Greek word *skotos*. One of the literal meanings of *skotos* is "darkened eyesight or blindness," and one of its figurative meanings is "ignorance respecting divine things." This says to me that the prince of this age is the ruler over the realm of ignorance. He has legal jurisdiction to operate in areas of people's lives—including the lives of believers—where they are ignorant of spiritual truths. The Bible puts it this way:

> My people are destroyed for lack of knowledge: because you have rejected knowledge, I will also reject you, that you shall be no priest to me: seeing you have forgotten the law of your God, I will also forget your children. (Hosea 4:6)

Multitudes of Christians all over the world have experienced the devastating effects of spiritual ignorance. Contrary to popular opinion, what you do not know *can* actually hurt you. Since the enemy of our souls rules in the realm of darkness, the more ignorance we walk in, the more powerful and fortified our adversary can become. In contrast, the more truth we walk in, the more light we walk in, the weaker our enemy's influence in our lives becomes.

The first time I experienced demonic oppression, I was completely ignorant of the enemy's devices. I knew almost nothing about the devil, and I definitely did not understand spiritual warfare. Even though I loved God and had a desire to know and serve Him, my life was being bombarded with demonic harassment in a particular area of my life, and I was oblivious to the truth that these spiritual attacks did not have to continue. After many months of satanic attacks against my mind and body, I finally began to understand that I could be free of the oppression, and I stood up to resist the enemy. The Bible says, "*Submit yourselves therefore to God. Resist the devil, and he will flee from you*" (James 4:7), and that is exactly what I did! When I submitted to God's Word in that area of my life, I was able to resist the enemy—and he fled!

Yes, the enemy of our souls dwells in darkness and hides behind veils of secrecy. Yet the moment we receive revelation about his destructive works, bring our sin or ignorance to God, repent of it, and stand upon the deliverance Jesus has provided for us, we break the enemy's power in our lives. Remember, before we can resist the devil, we must submit to God. How do we submit to Him? By willingly yielding ourselves to the truth of His Word. God's truth always exposes the enemy's lies.

I will never forget a story I heard about an actress who visited a medium and asked to consult with a deceased actor. After this consultation, the actress began to have visitations from the late actor in her bedroom. He would literally appear in her room at night and speak to her, giving her advice on what to do to advance her career. He would even relay to her the people she should connect with in order to reach her acting goals. As she heeded the advice, she became a very successful actress.

But, one day, she decided to veer away from the counsel of this deceased actor. Then everything changed. Instead of giving her advice, he threatened to destroy her. When that happened, she realized she was not dealing with the late actor at all but with an evil spirit. This demon began to torment her and even afflict her with infirmity. She finally cried out to God and surrendered her life to Jesus. Once she repented and turned to the Lord, she was delivered from the power of that familiar spirit.

Similar scenarios have happened time and time again. I heard another story of a woman who claimed to receive direction from her deceased child, saying that the child told her what to do every day. This woman began to experience confusion, lack, and great calamity in her life. Why was this happening? Because she was actually getting advice from a demonic spirit. I assure you, demons will never lead you to a good place!

Years ago, a young woman told me that her children were being tormented by ghosts in her house. The children would literally see poltergeists—apparitions or spirits—moving in and out of the walls of their home. Finally, this woman got a hold of my teaching on spiritual warfare and was able to minister deliverance to her children. Both she and her children were totally set free by the power of God. Hallelujah!

Many people around the world see entities in their rooms at night or hear voices. As much as we would like to think that such occurrences are simply the products of the active imaginations of a few frightened children, the reality is that there are legitimate accounts of people who have encountered familiar spirits in this way. How could people from various parts of the world, who speak different languages and have had different upbringings, see exactly the same things?

These experiences are not from God but are caused by demonic spirits. The spirits may impersonate people's deceased loved ones. They may visit individuals in dreams and visions, ultimately seeking to gain access to their lives and/or the lives of their family members.

TERRITORIAL SPIRITS

It is important to understand that principalities and demonic spirits are territorial in nature. They are often called "territorial spirits." Demons are not omnipresent (they cannot be everywhere at the same time); therefore, familiar spirits are assigned to various countries, regions, states, parishes, cities, townships, and communities. In my travels, I have found that particular countries or cities are under the influence of certain demonic strongholds. This is due to the fact that the people in authority in those places have come into covenants and agreements with the demonic powers, which grant them access to the cultures and the people.

A perfect biblical example of this reality may be seen in the ministry of the apostle Paul:

> And it came to pass, as we went to prayer, a certain damsel possessed with a spirit of divination met us, which brought her masters much gain by soothsaying: the same followed Paul and us, and cried, saying, These men are the servants of the Most High God, which show to us the way of salvation. And this did she many days. But Paul, being grieved, turned and said to the spirit, I command you in the name of Jesus Christ to come out of her. And he came out the same hour.
>
> (Acts 16:16–18)

When Paul and his fellow worker Silas traveled to Thyatira, they encountered a female slave with a *"spirit of divination."* This was a familiar spirit. The slave woman was possessed or otherwise under the power of this spirit, which enabled her to predict the future. The Greek word translated "*divination*" here is *pythōn*, from which we derive the English word *python*.[2] "In Greek mythology, [Python was] the name of the Pythian serpent or dragon that dwelt in the region of Pytho at the foot of Parnassus in Phocis, and was said to have guarded the oracle at Delphi and been slain by Apollo."[3]

The "*spirit of divination*" that Paul and Silas encountered was a territorial, serpentine spirit that controlled people and gave them false spiritual gifting. Paul and Silas did not encounter this spirit until they came into its geographical territory. Then, when Paul confronted and expelled the spirit, the entire region was affected economically because the slave woman lost her ability to tell the future. The gain that she had brought her masters through soothsaying was cut off. Paul and Silas experienced severe backlash and persecution because many people in the region were under the influence of this python spirit.

Every time a demonic spirit is cast out or a demonic power is broken, the effects of that demonic power are also broken. The enemy does not want people to be truly set free because, once they experience freedom, he loses his grip on them and the communities they influence. This is why it is so important that we receive the illumination of God's Word in our lives. The Word of God is the light that pierces the darkness and exposes Satan's activities. Ultimately, the slave woman was delivered and Paul and Silas were supernaturally released from prison after being beaten and jailed for disrupting the occult practices of the city. (See Acts 16:19–40.)

THE WORD OF GOD IS THE LIGHT THAT PIERCES THE DARKNESS AND EXPOSES SATAN'S ACTIVITIES.

2. *Merriam-Webster.com Dictionary*, s.v. "python," https://www.merriam-webster.com/dictionary/python.
3. See *Strong's Exhaustive Concordance of the Bible*, G4436, https://www.biblestudytools.com/lexicons/greek/kjv/puthon.html.

UNKNOWINGLY INVITING FAMILIAR SPIRITS

There are many ways we can unknowingly invite familiar spirits into our lives. We may leave open a door to their influence due to personal trauma, unforgiveness, bitterness, or false thinking. Then we become trapped in a type of spiritual debt. This debt restricts us from being fully free in Christ. That is why so many people feel like they are fighting invisible battles with unseen forces that hinder them.

Beloved, we must desire to live in the light and truth of our God, the only living God, who is our Creator and to whom we belong as Christian believers. We should desire to live out fully everything that Jesus attained for us on the cross. We are seated in heavenly places with Christ (see Ephesians 2:6), and we have victory over the lies of Satan. Therefore, we must choose to expose the enemy in every way he shows up in our lives and communities. We must come out of our spiritual ignorance by becoming knowledgeable about God's Word and learning to break the demonic curses that Christ has already paid in full for us to be released from.

In the church, there has often been a strong focus on behavioral modification but not enough emphasis on the truth that God wants us to walk in *total freedom*. He wants us to be set free from guilt, shame, condemnation, and the oppression of demonic spirits. You may be thinking to yourself, "Is it really possible to walk in total freedom? After all, everyone struggles with certain things. There is no way we can be totally delivered on this side of eternity, right?" Wrong! Yes, we must walk out the process of growing in Christlikeness through the power of the Holy Spirit, and this is a lifelong process. However, God does not want us to accept a lifestyle of affliction and bondage as normal.

Do you know people—including yourself—who feel like "something" is blocking them from moving forward in life?

Have you heard stories about people being attacked in their sleep by something or someone?

Have you ever felt a disturbing presence in your room or seen something that you cannot explain?

Whatever has been oppressing you and your loved ones must loosen its hold on you right now, in the name of Jesus! *Overcoming Familiar Spirits* will help to remove the veils concealing the familiar spirits that have been attacking you from the shadows. It will lead you into the manifestation of God's divine, peaceful, abundant purpose for your life.

PRAYER OF RELEASE

Heavenly Father, I thank You for having a divine purpose for my life and for providing me with lasting freedom through Jesus Christ. I no longer want pain, confusion, chaos, or havoc caused by the enemy to run my life. Because of Jesus's sacrifice, and in the power of the Spirit, I come against the familiar spirits that are hiding unseen and undetected in my mind and emotions. I rebuke any familiar spirits that have operated in secrecy in my life. Any unclean spirit that is attached to me, my home, or my bloodline must go! I declare that I am no longer oppressed by these demons on assignment. I give these destructive spirits *no place*. All forms of oppression that have infiltrated my belief system must loosen their hold on me right now! I thank You, Father, that my spiritual vision is restored. In Jesus's name, amen!

INSIGHTS FOR OVERCOMING

1. What are familiar spirits, and what is their origin?
2. Why are they called "familiar" spirits?
3. In what ways do familiar spirits operate?
4. How can we unknowingly invite familiar spirits into our lives?

ASK YOURSELF

1. In what areas of my life am I experiencing bondage to guilt, shame, or defeat?
2. What aspects of my belief system (such as my faith in God's goodness and in the trustworthiness of His Word) are being compromised by constant confusion or chaos?
3. Am I ready to be set free from spiritual oppression and bondage?

2

SPIRITUAL DEBT COLLECTORS

"And his lord was angry, and delivered him to the tormentors, till he should pay all that was due to him."
—Matthew 18:34

Has someone you know ever been threatened with legal action by a debt collector because they owed money but were having a difficult time paying it back? Have you ever personally had the uncomfortable experience of being repeatedly called by a debt collector over a certain outstanding bill?

A debt collector is a person or a company that regularly seeks to collect money, on behalf of a third party, on debts that people owe, usually when those debts are past due. The regulations that govern the actions of debt collectors vary from state to state and from country to country. In America, companies have the legal right to collect a debt when a person breaches a contractual agreement and becomes delinquent on an account or a financial obligation they had previously agreed to pay. In many cases, debt collectors will continue to pursue the debt until it is paid, discharged, or forgiven.

SPIRITUAL DEBT

Familiar spirits are like debt collectors because they pursue people who are in breach of spiritual covenants or agreements and have fallen into "spiritual debt." They are empowered to do this because, in one way or another, they have a legal claim to that debt in the spiritual realm. In other words, familiar spirits seek to identify a spiritual debt or legal breach, and then they execute their wicked agendas against the ignorant souls who have—often unknowingly—incurred these debts.

The English word *debt* comes from the Latin *debitum*, which means "something owed."[4] "Debt" simply refers to an amount that is past due or owed. In the natural world, when there is an outstanding debt, it means that someone has failed to pay something they were responsible for reimbursing. The person who owes is required to discharge that debt when there are legal grounds to obligate them to pay it.

Suppose a person goes to a loan shark to borrow money in order to keep their house from foreclosing. Now consider the specific terms that would be agreed upon between the loan shark and the person needing the money. It would not be unreasonable to assume that the borrower is in a desperate state and would probably not stop to consider how unfavorable the terms would be when dealing with a loan shark. The agreement would state certain consequences of a failure to repay the loan, such as drawing on the money the borrower had in their bank account, even if it was everything they had left. And after all that, their house might still go into foreclosure. However, sometimes the consequences might be even worse: a henchman might be deployed by the loan shark to collect the money that is owed, using physical force to "persuade" the borrower to repay the debt by whatever means possible.

> WHEN PEOPLE HAVE, IN ONE WAY OR ANOTHER, VIOLATED THEIR COVENANT WITH GOD AND COME INTO AGREEMENT WITH DEMONIC POWERS, THEY CAN UNKNOWINGLY OPEN THEMSELVES TO SPIRITUAL DEBT AND, CONSEQUENTLY, TO SATANIC DEBT COLLECTORS.

In the spiritual realm, many believers are seeing demonic attacks and even bondage on their lives or the lives of their loved ones because of oppressive "spiritual debt" they have incurred. When people have, in one way or

---

4. Lexico.com, s.v. "debt," https://www.lexico.com/en/definition/debt.

another, violated their covenant with God and come into agreement with demonic powers, they can unknowingly open themselves to such spiritual debt and, consequently, to satanic debt collectors. Throughout this book, I discuss different forms of spiritual debt and its causes, demonstrating how to identify those debts and have them discharged or released so you can live in freedom.

DEMONIC LIENS

Another way to look at spiritual debt is through the concept of liens. In general, a *lien* is defined as "a right to keep possession of property belonging to another person until a debt owed by that person is discharged."[5] A close friend of mine who is a very successful attorney specializing in real estate law once advised me regarding a potential real estate transaction I was involved in. As I talked with him about a property we were in the process of purchasing for our ministry, I told him that it was free and clear according to the owner's written declaration; in other words, there was no mortgage on it. However, my savvy attorney friend told me to do a title search before purchasing the property. He explained that even though the property might be debt free, it could still have a lien on it.

For instance, there is something called a mechanic's lien, which is a legal document that essentially reserves the right for people to file a suit seeking unpaid compensation in relation to the property. Such suits are usually filed by contractors, subcontractors, or suppliers who never received payment for work they performed or materials they provided. A mechanic's lien can prohibit the transference of a title from one party to another in the case of the potential sale or donation of the property. Though this advice from my attorney friend was insightful and helpful for the real estate transaction, it also provided me with an even greater understanding of spiritual warfare, particularly with regard to familiar spirits.

Just as there are liens in the natural world, there are liens in the spiritual realm. God showed me that many believers are subject to demonic liens, and this is why certain things that should be happening in their lives cannot happen. This is why some women have been praying for years about wanting a spouse, but they cannot get married. This is why some couples

5. Lexico.com, s.v. "lien," https://www.lexico.com/definition/lien.

have been praying for children, but the wives are unable to conceive. This is why some people's lives and ministries cannot gain enough momentum to get off the ground. A familiar spirit has infiltrated an area of their lives, and it must be removed through spiritual force.

Thus, when spiritual liens against you and/or your bloodline go unaddressed, this can create an opportunity for demonic spirits to attach themselves to your life and destiny. But God desires for you to be free of oppression and bondage in every area of your life. I don't know about you, but I want to live a debt-free life—not only materially but also spiritually! The Bible says,

> The rich rules over the poor, and the borrower is servant to the lender.
> (Proverbs 22:7)

Whenever a person is in debt, they are enslaved to the one they are indebted to. We are called to be the bondservants of Christ alone, not the servants of the devil, sin, or our emotions. Jesus paid our debt in full and released us from the curse and penalty of sin. But, again, Satan, *"the accuser of our brethren"* (Revelation 12:10), can place liens on the lives and destinies of God's people when they have, in some way, participated in iniquitous contracts and ungodly covenants. Even though a person is born again, they can still be afflicted by familiar spirits because they have unknowingly (and sometimes knowingly) come into agreement with satanic powers.

DEMONIC ACCESS POINTS

What types of scenarios lead to our being oppressed by spiritual debt collectors and demonic liens? They occur when we have open doors or portals in our lives that leave us vulnerable. A "portal" may be defined as "a doorway, gate, or other entrance, especially a large and imposing one."[6] Simply put, portals are spiritual open doors that give demons entrance. The enemy of our souls attempts to exploit access points and "legal loopholes" that allow him to execute his agenda in our lives.

I grew up in Georgia where the summers are very hot. In fact, there were times when the heat felt unbearable to me. I particularly remember

---

6. Lexico.com, s.v. "portal," https://www.lexico.com/definition/portal.

the hot and humid summer nights, which typically coincided with mosquito season. Honestly, when we stood outside, it felt like we were being bitten by a horde of flesh-eating vampires. To try to keep the mosquitoes away from us, we would slap our legs and arms so often and so loudly that it sounded like a percussion band! During that season, I would invariably hear the infamous shout from my mother or grandmother, "Close the door! You are letting bugs into the house!" At an early age, I learned the importance of closing the doors to the house so as not to allow "unwanted guests" inside. As simple as this analogy may seem, it teaches a very powerful and important spiritual lesson: do not leave the doors to your life open to demonic influence and oppression.

All demonic access points are the result of sin of some type. This may be sin we initiate ourselves, or it may be sin others commit against us that causes us to become susceptible to satanic oppression because we subsequently fall into woundedness or bitterness. There are other doors, including personal trauma and ignorance, that may lead to demonic portals. In coming chapters, we will be looking at various types of access points. However, since sin—whether willful or inadvertent; whether of commission or omission—is involved in most of the areas we will be discussing, in this chapter, we will explore the specific relationship between "the law of spiritual jurisdiction," the impact of sin, and the influence of familiar spirits.

SPIRITUAL JURISDICTION

If we don't understand the legalities of the spiritual realm, we can never successfully engage in spiritual warfare and overcome familiar spirits. The spiritual realm is governed by spiritual laws and protocols, and one of the first spiritual laws we must understand is the law of jurisdiction. The word *jurisdiction* means "the official power to make legal decisions and judgments," "the extent of the power to make legal decisions and judgments," or "a system of law courts; a judicature." The word is derived etymologically from the combination of two Latin words, *jur* (law) and *dictio* (saying).[7]

---

7. Lexico.com, s.v. "jurisdiction," https://www.lexico.com/definition/jurisdiction.

Human beings were given legal jurisdiction in the garden of Eden before the fall of mankind:

And God said, Let Us make man in Our image, after Our likeness: and let them have dominion over the fish of the sea, and over the fowl of the air, and over the cattle, and over all the earth, and over every creeping thing that creeps upon the earth. (Genesis 1:26)

And the LORD *God took the man, and put him into the garden of Eden to dress it and to keep it. And the* LORD *God commanded the man, saying, Of every tree of the garden you may freely eat: but of the tree of the knowledge of good and evil, you shall not eat of it: for in the day that you eat thereof you shall surely die.* (Genesis 2:15–17)

Even though human beings were given dominion by God, their dominion had a jurisdiction: the parameters God had given them. As long as they were living according to God's will and purpose in the garden of Eden, there was no creature on planet earth with more power or authority. Contrary to popular belief, mankind did not evolve through natural selection; we were specifically created and given authority by our Creator. However, from the moment Adam and Eve violated the law of jurisdiction by listening to the voice of the serpent (the devil) and disobeying God's direct instructions by eating from the Tree of Knowledge of Good and Evil, everything changed. When they committed high treason against the King of the universe, they allowed the enemy to strip them of their spiritual authority and rob them of their intimacy with God. The moment they sinned, the spirit of fear came into their lives, and they tried to run away from God's presence. (See Genesis 3:1–13.) The portal to demonic influence had been opened.

THE SPIRITUAL REALM IS GOVERNED BY SPIRITUAL LAWS AND PROTOCOLS, AND ONE OF THE FIRST SPIRITUAL LAWS WE MUST UNDERSTAND IS THE LAW OF JURISDICTION.

THE DOOR OF SIN

And the LORD *God said to the serpent, Because you have done this, you are cursed above all cattle, and above every beast of the field; upon your belly shall you go, and dust shall you eat all the days of your life: and I will put enmity between you and the woman, and between your seed and her seed; it shall bruise your head, and you shall bruise his heel. To the woman He said, I will greatly multiply your sorrow and your conception; in sorrow you shall bring forth children; and your desire shall be to your husband, and he shall rule over you. And to Adam He said, Because you have hearkened to the voice of your wife, and have eaten of the tree, of which I commanded you, saying, You shall not eat of it: cursed is the ground for your sake; in sorrow shall you eat of it all the days of your life; thorns also and thistles shall it bring forth to you; and you shall eat the herb of the field; in the sweat of your face shall you eat bread, till you return to the ground; for out of it were you taken: for dust you are, and to dust shall you return.*

(Genesis 3:14–19)

Notice that as a result of their sin, a curse entered into the lives of human beings and into the world in general. (See also Romans 5:12–14; 8:19–23.) But God had a plan of redemption already in place! (See Genesis 3:15.) The Bible says that the Lamb, Jesus, was slain before the foundation of the world. (See Revelation 13:8.) Jesus had to enter the earth as a human being through the womb of Mary. This gave Him legal grounds to operate in the earthly realm as the Son of Man. The way God designed the earth, spirits need bodies to legally operate in the world. Because God is a Spirit, He required a physical body in order to redeem humanity; hence, the incarnation of Christ. Thank God for His plan of redemption!

Why is all this important to understand? Jesus's work of redemption was not simply to save our souls from sin—as momentous as that work was—*but to reinstate our spiritual jurisdiction.* Because of what Jesus accomplished on the cross, we have authority and jurisdiction over the enemy once more. In other words, we have the official power to make legal decisions and judgments based on spiritual realities and spiritual laws. Guess who knows this? Satan does! This is why he works tirelessly to get us to abdicate our authority again through sin and ignorance. Our enemy understands well the legalities of the spiritual realm and the effects of sin.

SIN THE TASKMASTER

Jesus stated, "*Verily, verily, I say to you, Whosoever commits sin is the servant of sin*" (John 8:34). The word "*servant*" here comes from the Greek word *doulos*, which literally means "slave," "bond servant," or "bondman." A bondman is an indentured servant who labors for a certain period of time to pay off their master for contracted expenses, such as travel to work in another region or country, and room and board.[8]

When we operate in sin, we violate spiritual laws and open our lives to spiritual debt, and this debt, in turn, attracts demonic debt collectors and can even result in spiritual slavery or servanthood. The reality of our spiritual debt is central to the purpose of Jesus's sacrifice. His death on the cross in our place released the human race from its debt to sin, a concept we will explore more fully later in this chapter.

Jesus taught us that whoever commits sin is the servant or slave of sin. This is a very powerful statement, but it is much more complex than we often realize. Jesus was not just talking about someone making a mistake and doing something wrong. He was talking about someone engaging in deliberate, willful, continual sin. The Greek word translated "*commits*" in John 8:34 is *poieō*, among whose various meanings are "to make," "to acquire," "to constitute," "to carry out," "to execute," and "to perform."

Willful, unrepentant sin is the most potent means of demonic powers entering the lives of believers. In fact, it is a magnetic force for familiar spirits. Willful sin is risky and dangerous for us because it keeps us from having sustained victory in Christ. Therefore, when we persist in unrepentant sin, we are opening the door to evil spirits. Not only does unrepentant sin open the door, but, as I previously mentioned, it also causes spiritual agreements to form, granting demonic powers legal rights to withhold, delay, suppress, oppress, hinder, or stop the free flow of our spiritual destinies.

Jesus is saying that if we enter into an agreement with sin, then sin will become our slave master. For example, if you engage in an illicit relationship

---

8. *Merriam-Webster.com Dictionary*, s.v. "indentured servant," https://www.merriam-webster.com/dictionary/indentured%20servant.

with someone, whatever demonic oppression is upon that person's life has legal access to you. (See 1 Corinthians 6:16.) Someone who enters into a sexual relationship outside of marriage may suddenly start to feel depressed and suicidal, even though these are not their own feelings. It is because a spirit of suicide is attached to their sexual partner. Such a spiritual legal attachment can be perpetuated for years. Until this legal claim is released, it can follow people throughout their lives and even influence their children and subsequent generations. The only way it can be lifted is through revelation (understanding what is occurring in the spiritual realm), repentance, and receiving the atoning sacrifice of Jesus on their behalf.

WILLFUL, UNREPENTANT SIN IS THE MOST POTENT MEANS OF DEMONIC POWERS ENTERING THE LIVES OF BELIEVERS.

The Scriptures tell us:

Whosoever commits sin transgresses also the law: for sin is the transgression of the law. (1 John 3:4)

Then when lust hath conceived, it brings forth sin: and sin, when it is finished, brings forth death. (James 1:15)

The wages of sin is death; but the gift of God is eternal life through Jesus Christ our Lord. (Romans 6:23)

Because of Adam and Eve's sin, Satan had the legal grounds to collect the debt and ultimately administer death to mankind as a spiritual consequence of their sin. This penalty of death began with the first human beings but was applicable to the entire human race. This is why there is sickness, poverty, oppression, and death in the world today. But it was never God's original design for mankind to be afflicted with those consequences or any other kind of suffering. Romans 5:8 says,

But God commends his love toward us, in that, while we were yet sin-ners, Christ died for us.

Jesus died on the cross in our place to atone for our sins as the only acceptable, substitutionary sacrifice and to remove the sentence of con-demnation that was against us. He released the debt we owed through the efficacy of His blood. When we place our faith and trust in Him and repent of our sins, we receive forgiveness and are released from the debt.

"CROUCHING TIGER, HIDDEN DRAGON"

He that digs a pit shall fall into it; and whoso breaks a hedge, a serpent shall bite him.   (Ecclesiastes 10:8)

Let's look at the principle of legal access a little more closely. As I wrote earlier, some theologians believe demonic powers were present in the earth before human beings fell into sin. However, these demonic spirits did not have any legal rights to interfere with humanity until Adam and Eve ate from the Tree of Knowledge of Good and Evil. There is no record that Adam or Eve committed any additional rebellious acts against God after their fall in the garden of Eden. Yet human beings lost their fellowship and communion with the Creator from that point on. This loss of fellowship with God became the basis of humankind's spiritual depravity. By the time we get to Cain and Abel in Genesis 4, mankind had become so degenerate in just one generation that Cain murdered his brother. Sin opened the door to the spirit of murder. As the Lord told Cain,

If you do well, will you not be accepted? And if you do not do well, sin is couching ["lies" KJV, KJVER] at the door; its desire is for you, but you must master it.   (Genesis 4:7 RSV)

The word *"couching"* in the *Revised Standard Version* or *"lies"* in the King James Version is translated from the Hebrew word *rābas*, which means "to crouch (on all four legs folded, like a recumbent animal); by implication to recline, repose, brood, lurk."[9] Sin was crouching at the door of Cain's life, looking for a way in. And it found a legal entrance—*envy*. Cain's envy

---

9. *Strong's Exhaustive Concordance of the Bible,* STRONG, © 1980, 1986, and assigned to World Bible Publishers, Inc.

toward his brother, Abel, led to a spirit of jealousy, and this jealousy ultimately led to murder.

A profound spiritual law may be drawn from this passage of Scripture. Spiritual forces work by the law of invitation, a concept we will explore in more detail in later chapters. Despite His infinite power and sovereignty, God has chosen not to move on the earth without human invitation. You may be thinking, "But He is God—He can do whatever He wants." You are absolutely right! And He wants to operate by invitation. He does not desire to force Himself upon us or nullify the will He has given us. But God is not the only one desiring an invitation to come into our lives. Demonic powers are also governed by the spiritual law of invitation. Contrary to popular belief, Satan cannot do whatever he wants or arbitrarily enter people's lives and circumstances. He can only go where he is invited or where accommodation has been made for him. The enemy of our souls is constantly looking for such an opening.

Years ago, a movie was released called *Crouching Tiger, Hidden Dragon*. Although it was a martial arts fantasy/action film, I believe the title fits our discussion about familiar spirits. The accuser is like a "crouching lion" and a "hidden dragon." He is constantly lurking, out of sight, at the door to our lives. This is why the apostle Paul wrote,

Neither give place to the devil.   (Ephesians 4:27)

Again, the enemy can only go where he is invited or where an accommodation of some sort has been made for him. The Bible says, *"Be sober, be vigilant; because your adversary the devil, as a roaring lion, walks about, seeking whom he may devour"* (1 Peter 5:8). This verse is another very interesting and profound statement. First, let's look at the word *"adversary."* It is translated from the Greek word *antidikos*, one of the meanings of which is "an opponent in a suit of law." Satan is an opponent who seeks legal claims against the people of God. The devil is a professional litigant. He *"walks about"* seeking spiritual damages from those who are not vigilant and who are outside of the will and Word of God.

The phrase *"walks about"* is rendered from the Greek word *peripateō*, among whose meanings is "to make due use of opportunities." The devil is an opportunist; he cannot go after everyone or every situation, so he looks for opportunities that have been left open for him to exploit. It is similar to a person who goes around filing lawsuits every week. They look for a spill on the floor at the grocery store or the next car accident. They lie in wait for an opportunity to bring an accusation that will cause them to receive recompense of some form. This is the nature of our enemy.

Satan knows that there is nothing he can do in your life without your permission. And this is why Paul admonished us to *give him no place*. We must be alert to the schemes and tactics of the wicked one. Many people would suggest that the devil needs God's permission to do anything, but the reality is that he needs *your* permission and agreement in order to carry out his diabolical plan in your life.

> **SATAN CANNOT DO WHATEVER HE WANTS OR ARBITRARILY ENTER PEOPLE'S LIVES AND CIRCUMSTANCES. HE CAN ONLY GO WHERE HE IS INVITED OR WHERE ACCOMMODATION HAS BEEN MADE FOR HIM.**

CONFESSION AND CLEANSING

Sin is the atmosphere where demonic spirits thrive because it is the same atmosphere in which the devil operates. Thus, when we are engaged in willful sin against God, it sets spiritual consequences in motion. That is why we must seek to live a lifestyle of holiness and repentance. If you know that there are areas of blatant and willful sin in your life, I encourage you to repent and turn away from those sins now. Confess your sins to God and ask Him to deliver you and heal you in those areas. Pray and ask the Holy Spirit to expose any area of hidden or secret sin in your life before the light of God's Word. God is compassionate and eager to forgive if we come to Him with a sincere heart of repentance. First John 1:9 tells us:

> *If we confess our sins, He is faithful and just to forgive us our sins, and to cleanse us from all unrighteousness.*

The Greek word translated *"confess"* is *homologeo*, which means "to say the same thing as another, i.e. to agree with, assent" or "to admit or declare one's self guilty of what one is accused of." Once we agree with God, we break the enemy's power. We must admit when we have missed the mark and turn to God in humility, faith, and repentance.

The moment you confess your sin to God (and, in some cases, confess your sin to those whom your actions have impacted) and turn away from that sin, you receive supernatural cleansing from guilt, shame, and condemnation—and the accuser is silenced. Let me be clear: our sins are forgiven by the efficacious, atoning sacrifice of Jesus on the cross. His blood was shed to cleanse us from unrighteousness. It is by grace alone that we overcome the power of sin. We can live above sin by relying on the grace of God and the power of the Holy Spirit.

THE LAW BRINGS DEATH, BUT THE SPIRIT GIVES LIFE

First John 1:5 says, *"This then is the message which we have heard of Him, and declare to you, that God is light, and in Him is no darkness at all."* To walk in darkness is to invite evil spirits. We must guard our hearts and our souls against the sway of sin. To recognize and receive God's grace, we must first understand that the Old Testament law was not given with the intent to bring life but to function as a guide for living within the confines of what was acceptable to God and to warn of the punishment for breaking that law.

> *If you will not observe to do all the words of this law that are written in this book, that you may fear this glorious and fearful name, THE LORD YOUR GOD; then the LORD will make your plagues wonderful, and the plagues of your seed, even great plagues, and of long continuance, and sore sicknesses, and of long continuance. Moreover He will bring upon you all the diseases of Egypt, which you were afraid of; and they shall cling to you. Also every sickness, and every plague which is not written in the book of this law, them will the LORD bring upon you, until you be destroyed. And you shall be left few in number, whereas you were as the stars of heaven for multitude; because you would not obey the voice of the LORD your God.* (Deuteronomy 28:58–62)

Ultimately, the law pointed to the need for the sacrifice of Christ on our behalf, which would bring us into a new and better covenant by faith in Him:

> *But before faith came, we were kept under the law, shut up to the faith which should afterwards be revealed. Wherefore the law was our schoolmaster to bring us to Christ, that we might be justified by faith. But after that faith is come, we are no longer under a schoolmaster. For you are all the children of God by faith in Christ Jesus. For as many of you as have been baptized into Christ have put on Christ.*
>
> (Galatians 3:23–27)

> *For the law was given by Moses, but grace and truth came by Jesus Christ.* (John 1:17)

Satan and his demons came to discourage, torment, harass, abuse, and ultimately destroy people by preventing them from receiving and walking in the abundant life God desires for them. Jesus came to provide an abundant life in the kingdom of God for all who believe in Him. In John 10:10, Jesus said,

> *The thief comes not, but for to steal, and to kill, and to destroy: I am come that they might have life, and that they might have it more abundantly.*

We have seen that when we willfully sin against God and disobey His Word—as a practice and a lifestyle—we invite spiritual darkness into our lives, making ourselves (and sometimes our loved ones) vulnerable to spiritual attacks and demonic oppression. This is not to say that every attack that comes against our lives is the result of something we did wrong or a sin that we have committed; however, we must understand that a failure to operate according to the Word of God can unnecessarily expose us to negative spiritual consequences. Sometimes, we don't realize that we are going against God's Word and leaving ourselves vulnerable. In coming chapters, we will explore some specific ways we can open demonic portals in our lives and how to close them again so we may live in peace and freedom. But first, we need to better understand our restored authority and jurisdiction as believers in Jesus Christ.

PRAYER OF RELEASE

Heavenly Father, thank You for releasing me of my debt to You as my Creator through the efficacy of the shed blood of Your Son, Jesus Christ. Because of Jesus, I am under a new covenant that gives me power and authority over Satan and familiar spirits. Therefore, I ask that You would forgive me for any ways in which I have violated my covenant with You and opened myself to spiritual debt. Forgive me for any areas of my life that I have not submitted to the Spirit of God out of stubbornness or self-will that have led to bondage through demonic agreements. And for any doors I may have unknowingly opened in my life, I ask the Holy Spirit to reveal those areas to me. Your Word says in Revelation 3:7 that Jesus is *"the one who has the key of David. What he opens, no one can close; and what he closes, no one can open."*[10] Therefore, I ask You, Lord, to close all doors to the demonic realm that I have illegally opened. I declare that I am free, by faith and through the blood of Jesus Christ! Amen.

INSIGHTS FOR OVERCOMING

1. Familiar spirits are like debt collectors because they pursue people who are in breach of spiritual covenants or agreements and have fallen into "spiritual debt."

2. Demonic liens cause people to continually struggle with the same hindrances and problems. The reason is that a familiar spirit has infiltrated an area of their lives, and it must be removed through spiritual force.

3. Willful, unrepentant sin is the most potent means of demonic powers entering the lives of believers.

---

10. NLT.

4. Jesus's work of redemption was not simply to save our souls from sin—as momentous as that work was—but to reinstate our spiritual jurisdiction and enable us to have victory over the enemy.

PRACTICUM

1. Write down areas in your life in which you desire to receive revelation from God about being released from spiritual debt and demonic liens.

2. As you receive further revelation and insight from God, pray and ask God's forgiveness for areas in which you have given the devil a foothold in your life.

3. Read and commit these verses to memory:

Verily, verily, I say to you, Whosoever commits sin is the servant of sin. (John 8:34)

Neither give place to the devil. (Ephesians 4:27)

If we confess our sins, He is faithful and just to forgive us our sins, and to cleanse us from all unrighteousness. (1 John 1:9)

3

THE AUTHORITY OF THE BELIEVER

"Behold, I give to you power to tread on serpents and scorpions,
and over all the power of the enemy:
and nothing shall by any means hurt you."
—Luke 10:19

As New Testament believers, we have been given supernatural authority to overcome familiar spirits through the name of Jesus and the power of the Holy Spirit. I can't emphasize this point enough. However, if we are going to successfully operate in this authority, we must understand the way authority works.

Imagine that a person is driving sixty-five miles per hour on a twenty-five-mile-per-hour street, and they are being pursued by the police. They would probably notice the flashing lights of the police car and slow down, pull over to the side of the road, roll down their window, and provide the officer with their driver's license and registration. The police officer would likely ask them if they knew the posted speed limit and question why they had been driving so fast.

Most reasonable people would cooperate with the officer, displaying a tremendous amount of respect. Why? Because of the police officer's legal authority. While there are some people who would not obey the instructions of the police, such individuals are, by far, the exception. Police officers have received delegated authority to confront, apprehend, and arrest those who break the law. If the individual violating the law does not respond to the badge of authority, the officer is empowered to use force to back up that authority. This will normally cause the person being confronted to comply with the officer's directives.

Now imagine a police officer who does not abide by the rule of law. They would compromise their ability to operate in their authority. If the officer were corrupt, turning a blind eye to crimes being committed and allowing lawbreakers to do as they pleased, that officer would be guilty of neglecting to execute and uphold the trust they had been given.

OPERATING IN SPIRITUAL POWER AND AUTHORITY

In many ways, we are like spiritual police officers. We have been given authority by Jesus Christ to confront, apprehend, and arrest demonic powers. And, when we are abiding by the rule of law in our spiritual lives, familiar spirits and other demonic powers recognize our authority.

Unlike natural police officers, the authority we carry is not backed by an earthly institution but by all of heaven! I will discuss this concept in more detail shortly. This does not mean that demonic powers won't continue to attempt to break spiritual laws or bring destruction to people's lives. But it does mean that, as believers, we have jurisdictional authority to confront these spirits and deal with them accordingly.

Remember, nothing can function—whether in a positive or a negative way—in our spiritual lives without our permission, and, for this reason, familiar spirits are constantly looking for permission to operate. Again, they can only operate in the areas of our lives where we grant them access. I have literally spoken to hundreds of thousands of people who are struggling with the oppression of demonic powers. Some of these demonic powers manifest in the form of sickness, while others manifest in the form of addiction, compulsion, or calamity. However, one thing is certain: if there is demonic activity (especially persistent activity), some form of agreement has been established in the spiritual realm—either on the part of the individual or on the part of someone who has influence in their lives. This agreement can be conscious or unconscious.

Many years ago, I spoke with a woman who was dealing with a chronic illness. She had been diagnosed with this sickness at a very young age, so she had lived with the condition for nearly her entire life. When she experienced an attack, she would often collapse as a result of the tremendous pain it inflicted. One day, I asked her if she desired to be whole. It was then that she realized she had come into agreement with a spirit of infirmity—a familiar spirit.

It is not uncommon for people with certain conditions to gather around, and build community with, others based on their shared afflictions. While I am an advocate of support groups, we must be careful not to build "community" around demons. Unfortunately, many people have unknowingly granted agreement to demonic entities because they have believed a narrative that was untrue and unscriptural. For example, they may think that their condition is chronic and hopeless. Beloved, this is a lie from the pit of darkness. You can be healed! You can be free! You can be whole in every area of your life. However, demons do not want you to believe this is possible or walk in this truth. They will torment, harass, oppress, and afflict in order to maintain their open door—the door of agreement.

WHEN WE ABIDE BY THE RULE OF LAW IN OUR SPIRITUAL LIVES, FAMILIAR SPIRITS AND OTHER DEMONIC POWERS RECOGNIZE OUR AUTHORITY.

FOUR PRINCIPLES FOR EXERCISING SPIRITUAL AUTHORITY

In order to exercise authority over demonic powers, we must understand and align our lives with four key spiritual principles. As with other truths, these principles overlap, but it is essential to recognize each aspect.

1. ALL AUTHORITY AND POWER HAVE A SOURCE

First, all authority and power have a source. The type and degree of authority and power is determined by its source. God is all encompassing, and therefore He is our number one source for everything we need for *"life and godliness"* (2 Peter 1:3).

Ultimately, all power comes from the spiritual realm, including life itself. In John 1:1–4, we read:

> *In the beginning was the Word, and the Word was with God, and the Word was God. The same was in the beginning with God. All things were made by Him; and without Him was not any thing made that was made. In Him was life; and the life was the light of men.*

As created beings, our very life was breathed into us by God. As the Scriptures tell us, *"For in Him we live, and move, and have our being"* (Acts 17:28). Therefore, any power that we operate in and through must come from God, who is the legal source of all things incorruptible. This power is obtained (received) through transference (connection). Where there is no connection, there is no power!

Imagine that one of your electrical appliances is disconnected from the power outlet, and it doesn't have any batteries inside. Now imagine that you press the "on" button to that appliance. What happens? You guessed it! Absolutely nothing. The same principle is true of our spiritual lives. If we attempt to operate in the spiritual power and authority that our heavenly Father has given us without maintaining a healthy connection to Him, that power and authority will have no potency. Jesus taught us:

> *Abide in Me, and I in you. As the branch cannot bear fruit of itself, except it abide in the vine; no more can you, except you abide in Me.*
> (John 15:4)

This verse points to the interconnection between the branch—us, as believers—and the Vine—Jesus, in His complete and divine personhood—as a necessity for us to walk in power. We have no life or power of our own. When we remain connected to God, "bearing fruit," or producing results for His kingdom, becomes inevitable. It is a supernatural consequence of being joined with the One who *is* life. It is impossible to come up empty if and when God is at the helm of your life.

2. AUTHORITY AND POWER ARE RECEIVED OR TRANSFERRED

Second, in connection with knowing that God is our ultimate source, we must understand that all true authority is received or transferred. As I mentioned earlier, we do not have any spiritual authority outside of Jesus. We have to experience a level of pressing, of revelation, that brings us to a place of conviction that, without Christ, we can do nothing. (See John 15:4.) Without *transference* from the one and only, all powerful, living God, we can have no real, sustainable power. In fact, if we operate in any supernatural or natural power that does not align with the Word of God, that power is illegal, illegitimate, and can bring people under submission to the influence of demonic spirits.

Contrary to what many believers think, sitting in a pew in a church is not a qualification for receiving God's power. How do we know this? There are many believers who have attended church for years but do not exercise—and perhaps have never exercised—God's power. They haven't experienced His power in their lives or seen it demonstrated within their families.

It is necessary that we first *receive* from God in order to operate from heaven. This does not have to do with attaining head knowledge about Him. Rather, it is a conscious revelation of the power of God flowing to us and through us because of the presence and work of the Holy Spirit in our lives. We must acknowledge the Spirit of God as the One who lives in us. Because of Him, we have supernatural capabilities and the conviction of *"Christ in you"* (Colossians 1:27) to operate in power and authority.

It is necessary for us to understand that familiar spirits cannot inhabit environments where God's presence and Spirit are hosted—dare I say— *continuously.* The great men of God in the book of Acts had to continually walk in spiritual victory to see kingdom results. It would have been difficult for them to have seen the sustained move of God if they hadn't yielded to His power and His way of doing things.

Just before Jesus ascended to heaven, He told His disciples to wait in Jerusalem until they had *received* heavenly power:

> *And, behold, I send the promise of My Father upon you: but tarry you in the city of Jerusalem, until you be endued with power from on high.*
> (Luke 24:49)

> *But you shall receive power, after that the Holy Ghost is come upon you: and you shall be witnesses to Me both in Jerusalem, and in all*

Judaea, and in Samaria, and to the uttermost part of the earth.

(Acts 1:8)

After Christ's resurrection, it was necessary for His followers to receive God's Spirit in order to be able to function in the same way He had when He walked on the earth. Acts 10:38 reminds us:

God anointed Jesus of Nazareth with the Holy Ghost and with power: who went about doing good, and healing all that were oppressed of the devil; for God was with Him.

The level of authority and power that is transferred is determined by the strength of what is delegated. In the Gospels, Jesus referred to delegated power when commissioning His disciples:

Behold, I give to you power to tread on serpents and scorpions, and over all the power of the enemy: and nothing shall by any means hurt you. (Luke 10:19)

And Jesus came and spoke to them, saying, All power is given to Me in heaven and in earth. Go you therefore, and teach all nations, baptizing them in the name of the Father, and of the Son, and of the Holy Ghost: teaching them to observe all things whatsoever I have commanded you: and, lo, I am with you always, even to the end of the world.

(Matthew 28:18–20)

Authority is delegated from one person (or government) to another. Delegated authority is the right to act on the behalf of the one who has the ultimate authority. Earlier, we talked about how, for the believer, Christ is the only legal access to power and authority. So, the spiritual authority that every Christian possesses comes from Jesus alone. We do not have any spiritual authority outside of Him.

Jesus was intentional about delegating His power and authority to His disciples, including us:

Verily, verily, I say to you, he that believes on Me, the works that I do shall he do also; and greater works than these shall he do; because I go to My Father. (John 14:12)

was a crack house across the street from my home. The people who occupied that crack house were engaged in trafficking and prostitution as well. One day, my mother-in-law asked me if I knew what was going on in that house. Of course, I knew what was going on, but I told her that we couldn't do anything about it. She quickly exclaimed, "I thought you had the authority!"

I was both shocked and challenged by her reply. I said to myself, "She is right! I do have the authority in Christ." That same day, I went to the edge of my porch and said, "In the name of Jesus, I declare that this house is shut down!" and then went back into my home. Two weeks later, the crack house was abandoned, and it was eventually condemned by the city. We never called a single governmental agency about the problem, although there is nothing wrong with calling the authorities. Instead, we dealt with the problem spiritually. Imagine what would happen if churches all over America began to declare with authority that the trafficking and prostitution and crack houses in their various cities would cease and desist!

AS JESUS'S FOLLOWERS, WE, TOO, HAVE BEEN GIVEN AUTHORITY "IN HEAVEN AND IN EARTH."

4. AUTHORITY AND POWER HAVE A COST

Fourth, we must be aware that there is a cost to operating in kingdom authority and power. It is not a passive stance. Authority only functions when you operate in the confines of the instruction of the one delegating it to you. This means we cannot be estranged from God's Manual, or Word, and maintain legal power to operate. If the enemy can disconnect us from our spiritual source, he can strip us of our power.

Christ Jesus was aware of and deliberate in acknowledging the source of His power:

Then answered Jesus and said to them, Verily, verily, I say to you, The Son can do nothing of Himself, but what He sees the Father do: for what things soever He does, these also does the Son likewise.

(John 5:19)

It is the case for millions of people that, even after receiving Christ and experiencing being born again, within a very short time, they become lukewarm or cold concerning the things of God. Why is that? There are various factors. Perhaps they were not discipled or did not maintain a connection with their local church (if they had one) and therefore fell into stagnation. I emphasize this because I know how easy it can be to stray from or become disconnected from God and the life of His Spirit.

It does not matter how ecstatic or illustrious our encounters with God may be, the accuser of the brethren is forever on a mission to divert our attention from the Creator so that we do not come into the full manifestation of His power in us. Remember that Satan's motivation is *"to steal, and to kill, and to destroy"* (John 10:10). Yes, there are costs to maintaining our relationship with God, such as vigilance and continually allowing His Word to conform us to the image of His Son. However, the costs are greater if we become estranged from God and His Word, as well as from the body of Christ.

Jesus always operated in the anointing for which He came to earth. But we must remember what it cost Jesus to redeem us. Christ's obedience to God the Father required Him to operate within the parameters the Father had given Him and to rely totally on the power of the Holy Spirit. Jesus not only paid a price of obedience and sacrifice throughout His three years of ministry, but He also paid the ultimate price—death on a cross. As a result, the Father set Him *"far above all principality, and power, and might, and dominion, and every name that is named, not only in this world, but also in that which is to come"* (Ephesians 1:21). Thank You, Jesus!

Because Jesus paid the full cost, died for our sins, and rose triumphantly, He is the One who is able to sustain and help us. You and I function from His power, not our own.

Now to Him that is able to do exceeding abundantly above all that we ask or think, according to the power that works in us.

(Ephesians 3:20)

It is Jesus's responsibility to save and deliver, and it is our responsibility to abide in Him. Again, it is His power that works in us when we stay connected to our source. That is why our stance in Christ has to be deliberate. We have to be available for Him to use us in His purposes; we must sacrifice our time and energy to read, study, and meditate on the Word of God; we need to operate as God wills and to surrender to His plans for our lives.

Christ lives in and through us to establish and operate the reality of God's kingdom here on earth:

> *For You* [Jesus, the Lamb] *were slain, and have redeemed us to God by Your blood out of every kindred, and tongue, and people, and nation; and have made us to our God kings and priests: and we shall reign on the earth.* (Revelation 5:9–10)

Each and every one of us has a calling on our lives. How we function within that calling depends upon our connection to the source of power— our deliberate yielding to God. Jesus said, *"For many are called, but few are chosen"* (Matthew 22:14). In order for us to walk in the manifestation of what Christ worked for us on the cross and by His resurrection, His authority and power must be evident in our lives.

You and I had to receive Christ before we could walk in His authority. When we accepted His shed blood on our behalf, when God gave us a measure of faith to answer the call to salvation and profess our commitment to Jesus, when we believed and received the gift of the indwelling Holy Spirit—all of these aspects were evidence that Jesus was calling us to Himself so that we could be a blessing to others under His authority and in the power of His Spirit.

> *To open their eyes, and to turn them from darkness to light, and from the power of Satan to God, that they may receive forgiveness of sins, and inheritance among them which are sanctified by faith that is in Me.* (Acts 26:18)

You have been given everything you need to live out the reality of your salvation, to go *"from faith to faith"* (Romans 1:17) and *"from glory to glory"* (2 Corinthians 3:18 NKJV), to walk out the calling of God on your life. Notice that I didn't say "to walk out your job." Your job is what you are *paid* for, but your calling is what you are *made* for. A set of freshly printed business cards with the title "Pastor" or "Apostle" or "Evangelist" is not what qualifies you for ministry. Obedience to God and His Word is what will bear supernatural fruit in your life. We dishonor God our Creator when we disobey His way of doing things. And whenever we dishonor our head, or authority, we lose influence. This is true not just of our relationship with God, but also of our relationships with human beings whom He has placed in authority over us to guide us in our natural and spiritual walks on earth.

Remember, in the book of Acts, the believers were able to do great works only because they were connected to their Source. Their works were always in keeping with the parameters of the gospel they had received and the power of the Holy Spirit working in them. Paul wrote,

> *For the kingdom of God is not in word, but in power.*
> (1 Corinthians 4:20)

> *…through mighty signs and wonders, by the power of the Spirit of God; so that from Jerusalem, and round about unto Illyricum, I have fully preached the gospel of Christ.* (Romans 15:19)

OBEDIENCE TO GOD AND HIS WORD IS WHAT WILL BEAR SUPERNATURAL FRUIT IN YOUR LIFE.

STAY UNDER GOD'S PROTECTION

To conclude this chapter on the believer's authority, I want to emphasize again that anything from the spiritual realm needs permission to freely operate on the physical earth. We must continually stay obedient to God and under His protection to have authority over familiar spirits—both to prevent them from infiltrating our lives in the first place and to regain our authority over them after we have given them an opening.

In Numbers 22, there is a very interesting story of a backslidden prophet named Balaam whose prophetic ministry became contaminated by his love of money. People with a prophetic gifting on their lives must be particularly careful not to defile themselves by a love of money. This story is also a very detailed example of how familiar spirits operate.

> [King Balak of Moab] *sent messengers therefore to Balaam the son of Beor to Pethor, which is by the river of the land of the children of his people, to call him, saying, Behold, there is a people come out from Egypt: behold, they cover the face of the earth, and they abide opposite me: come now therefore, I pray you, curse me this people; for they are too mighty for me: perhaps I shall prevail, that we may smite them, and that I may drive them out of the land: for I know that he whom you bless is blessed, and he whom you curse is cursed. And the elders of Moab and the elders of Midian departed with the rewards of divination in their hand; and they came to Balaam, and spoke to him the words of Balak.* (Numbers 22:5–7)

King Balak of Moab was intimidated by the Israelites, so he wanted them destroyed. He knew Balaam was an accurate prophet, and he wanted to pay Balaam a handsome sum of money in order to decree a curse over God's people. In the ancient world, curses were verbal pronouncements or imprecations that could carry spiritual authority. Such curses would set spiritual forces in motion that could cause ill favor, sickness, calamity, destruction, and/or even death.

It is very important to understand that pagan nations such as the Moabites were in agreement with, and under the authority of, demonic powers. They hated Israel because of the spirits that were controlling them. King Balak did not have the spiritual authority to curse the Israelites himself, so he sought to hire Balaam to do his dirty work. Of course, if you are familiar with this story, you know that things did not go according to King Balak's plan. Instead of cursing the Israelites, Balaam blessed them, later saying, *"How shall I curse, whom God has not cursed? or how shall I defy, whom the LORD has not defied?"* (Numbers 23:8).

The twist in the story comes two chapters later, in Numbers 25:

And Israel abode in Shittim, and the people began to commit whoredom with the daughters of Moab. And they called the people to the sacrifices of their gods: and the people did eat, and bowed down to their gods. And Israel joined himself to Baal-peor: and the anger of the LORD was kindled against Israel. (Numbers 25:1–3)

Even though King Balak had not been able to curse the Israelites through divine imprecation, the Israelites brought a curse upon themselves by violating spiritual laws. Many of the men married Moabite women, thus inviting familiar spirits to defile their people. They participated in idolatrous practices. They entered into a covenant with the very people who had been hell-bent on destroying them; by doing so, they opened the door to spiritual consequences and provoked God to judge them. This is what God told Moses to do to those involved in worshipping Baal-peor:

Take all the heads of the people, and hang them up before the LORD against the sun, that the fierce anger of the LORD may be turned away from Israel. And Moses said to the judges of Israel, Slay you every one his men that were joined to Baal-peor. (Numbers 25:4–5)

Wow! This sequence of events is a profound revelation about spiritual warfare. The Moabites represent demonic powers. They worshipped demons disguised as deities. They performed evil rituals and defiled the land they inhabited. Again, their association with demonic powers is why they were always hostile toward the Israelites. Note that when the Israelites operated under divine protection, their enemies could not successfully curse them. However, when they went out from under that protection, they were susceptible to the curse.

The accuser of the brethren does not care how you experience destruction—whether it is by self-condemnation, spiritual oppression, or judgment—as long as he can establish a legal accusation in the spiritual realm. The apostle Paul urged the Romans:

Neither yield you your members as instruments of unrighteousness to sin: but yield yourselves to God, as those that are alive from the dead, and your members as instruments of righteousness to God.... Know you not, that to whom you yield yourselves servants to obey, his servants *you are to whom you obey; whether of sin to death, or of obedience to righteousness?... I speak after the manner of men because of the infirmity of your flesh: for as you have yielded your members servants to uncleanness and to iniquity to iniquity; **even so now yield your members servants to righteousness to holiness.*** (Romans 6:13, 16, 19)

One dictionary definition of the verb *yield* is "to give way under force or pressure."[11] The Greek word translated *"yield"* in the above passage is *paristēmi*. In a literal sense, several of its meanings are "to place beside or near," "to set at hand," "to provide," "to place a person or thing at one's disposal," "to present or show," and "to bring to, bring near." Figuratively, the word can mean "to bring into one's fellowship or intimacy."

In the past, we may have unknowingly (or knowingly) yielded to the influence of familiar spirits. But now that we understand the nature of these wicked spirits and how they seek an invitation to infiltrate our lives, we can stop their oppression by actively yielding to God instead. We can repent and seek the Lord, committing ourselves to Him and to obeying His Word. Then He will restore our spiritual authority and power to defeat familiar spirits and expel them from our spiritual jurisdiction. Remember these words of Paul:

That you may know what is the hope of His calling, and what the riches of the glory of His inheritance in the saints, and what is the exceeding greatness of His power to us-ward who believe, according to the working of His mighty power. (Ephesians 1:18–19)

PRAYER OF RELEASE

Heavenly Father, thank You for the spiritual authority and power You have given me through Christ Jesus. You have granted me the ability to confront, apprehend, and arrest demonic powers. As long as I am abiding by the rule of law in my spiritual life, familiar spirits and other demonic powers will recognize my authority, and they can be stopped and expelled. I yield myself completely to You, and I ask You to help me align my life with the spiritual principles

---

11. Lexico.com, s.v. "yield," https://www.lexico.com/definition/yield.

of authority. I recognize You as the sole source of my authority and power. I ask You to help me, as the branch, to remain continually connected to You, the Vine. Let me recognize and submit to the power of the Holy Spirit flowing through me so that I can walk in victory in my own life and help build the kingdom of God on earth as it is in heaven: bringing healing, deliverance, and Your transforming love to everyone I meet. In Jesus's name, amen!

INSIGHTS FOR OVERCOMING

1. If we are going to successfully operate in spiritual authority, we must understand the way authority works.

2. We have been given authority by Jesus Christ to confront, apprehend, and arrest demonic powers. When we are abiding by the rule of law in our spiritual lives, familiar spirits and other demonic powers recognize our authority.

3. Because of the indwelling Holy Spirit, we have supernatural capabilities and the conviction of *"Christ in you"* (Colossians 1:27) to operate in power and authority.

4. In order to exercise authority over demonic powers, we must understand and align our lives with these four key spiritual principles: (1) all authority and power have a source; (2) authority and power are received or transferred; (3) authority and power are jurisdictional; (4) authority and power have a cost.

ASK YOURSELF

1. Am I operating in the spiritual authority Christ has provided for me? Why or why not?

2. Which of the four principles of spiritual authority do I especially need to move into alignment with at this time in my life?

3. If I have moved out from under God's authority, what steps can I take to yield to Him and be restored to my spiritual inheritance?

4

DEMONIC PORTALS: EMOTIONS AND THOUGHTS

"Finally, brethren, whatsoever things are true, whatsoever things are honest, whatsoever things are just, whatsoever things are pure, whatsoever things are lovely, whatsoever things are of good report; if there be any virtue, and if there be any praise, think on these things."
—Philippians 4:8

Now that we know our spiritual authority in Christ, we are ready to look more closely at the various doors that the enemy uses to find an entrance to our lives. To return to our earlier analogy, demonic powers are like mosquitoes that attempt to gain access in order to "feed" on believers. When we leave spiritual doors open through sin and ignorance, we allow these unwanted guests to attach themselves to our lives and cause confusion, frustration, havoc, sickness, calamity, destruction, despair, and even death.

Some of these demonic portals have similar elements, but each is important to discuss individually. In this chapter, we will explore demonic portals connected to our emotions and thoughts, and in chapter 5, we will examine portals related to curses and soul ties.

OFFENSE AND UNFORGIVENESS

One of the ways we open our lives to spiritual debt and demonic liens is through holding on to an offense and refusing to forgive others. In fact,

I believe offense or unforgiveness is the single greatest doorway to demonization and oppression. In my opinion, more familiar spirits are invited into people's lives through offense than by any other means. The apostle Paul wrote,

> Now I beseech you, brethren, mark them which cause divisions and offenses contrary to the doctrine which you have learned; and avoid them. (Romans 16:17)

Paul uses a very interesting Greek word for "offenses" in this verse—skandalon. This is the term from which the English word scandal was derived. Skandalon literally means "a trap," "a snare," or "any impediment placed in the way and causing one to stumble or fall, (a stumbling block, occasion of stumbling) i.e. a rock which is a cause of stumbling." This is a word picture of a fowler who sets a trap for his prey. Once the bird takes the bait, it is ensnared and ultimately killed. In other words, offense is a trap set by Satan to lead people into spiritual bondage and even spiritual death. Often, people do not understand the severity of the consequences of harboring offenses in their lives. But the consequences are so serious that Jesus taught us the following:

> Therefore if you bring your gift to the altar, and there remember that your brother has anything against you; leave there your gift before the altar, and go your way; first be reconciled to your brother, and then come and offer your gift. (Matthew 5:23–24)

Our Lord teaches us that offense can impede our worship and sacrifice. Demons also know this, and that is why familiar spirits are always seeking to set the stumbling block of offense before believers. An offended Christian is a bound Christian. When we remain offended by someone or something, it can lead to unforgiveness, bitterness, mental turmoil, spiritual weakness, and physical infirmity.

Often, when we think of a person being demonized, we picture someone rolling on the ground or barking like a dog, but there are much more insidious manifestations of demonic influence in a person's life. Diminished spiritual vision, an inability to hear the voice of God, continual cycles of sin and defeat, and a persistent feeling of torment are all signs that a person is under the influence of a familiar spirit or spirits. The key to experiencing freedom is to release the offense, no matter how justified it seems. You must make the conscious decision that you will no longer live under the bondage of the enemy.

We need to understand how unforgiveness can cause a legal claim to come against us in the spiritual realm. The Bible gives a very profound depiction of this. In the gospel of Matthew, chapter 18, Jesus teaches His disciples about the power and necessity of forgiveness:

> *Then came Peter to Him, and said, Lord, how often shall my brother sin against me, and I forgive him? till seven times? Jesus says to him, I say not to you, Until seven times: but, Until seventy times seven. Therefore is the kingdom of heaven likened to a certain king, which would take account of his servants. And when he had begun to reckon, one was brought to him, which owed him ten thousand talents. But forasmuch as he had not to pay, his lord commanded him to be sold, and his wife, and children, and all that he had, and payment to be made. The servant therefore fell down, and worshiped him, saying, Lord, have patience with me, and I will pay you all. Then the lord of that servant was moved with compassion, and loosed him, and forgave him the debt. But the same servant went out, and found one of his fellow servants, which owed him a hundred pence: and he laid hands on him, and took him by the throat, saying, Pay me that you owe. And his fellow servant fell down at his feet, and besought him, saying, Have patience with me, and I will pay you all. And he would not: but went and cast him into prison, till he should pay the debt. So when his fellow servants saw what was done, they were very sorry, and came and told to their lord all that was done. Then his lord, after that he had called him, said to him, O you wicked servant, I forgave you all that debt, because you desired me: should not you also have had compassion on your fellowservant, even as I had pity on you? And his lord was angry, and delivered him to the tormentors, till he should pay all that was due to him. So likewise shall My heavenly Father do also to you, if you from your hearts forgive not every one his brother their trespasses.* (Matthew 18:21–35)

Through this illustration, we see that, in the kingdom of God, a very powerful spiritual law called "the law of reciprocity" is in operation. The servant was forgiven a debt he was incapable of paying. Even if he worked for the remainder of his life, he would not be able to accumulate enough money to pay what he owed. In fact, his children probably would have inherited the debt after he died. Notice that the lord commanded that the man, his wife, and his children were to be sold into slavery. The man literally begged his master to have patience and grant an extension so he would be able to repay all the debt. Instead of extending the repayment schedule of the loan, the lord had compassion on this servant and forgave the debt in its entirety. The man was released from the debt completely, with no further obligation to repay. Therefore, the penalty of this debt was no longer enforceable. This is a very important spiritual principle.

However, instead of rejoicing and being thankful, the man immediately went to collect a debt that one of his fellow servants owed him. It is implied in the text that this debt was separate from the one the man was previously forgiven. Even though the fellow servant asked for grace and requested an extension of time (just as he had), he refused to show mercy and had the other man thrown into prison until he could repay the debt in full. This was the exact opposite of the grace the first servant had experienced. Of course, news of what happened reached his lord, and the lord became very angry. Notice this portion of the passage:

> *Then his lord, after that he had called him, said to him, O you wicked servant, I forgave you all that debt, because you desired me: should not you also have had compassion on your fellowservant, even as I had pity on you? And his lord was angry, and delivered him to the tormentors, till he should pay all that was due to him.* (Matthew 18:32–34)

"*His lord...delivered him to the tormentors, till he should pay all that was due to him.*" The word "*tormentors*" is translated from the Greek word *basanistēs*, which can mean "inquisitor" or "jailer"; it comes from a verb meaning "to torture" or "to vex." This term indicates the oppression and harassment of demonic powers. Because this servant broke a spiritual law, it opened the door to "debt collectors" in his life. His refusal to forgive his fellow servant brought him back under the law and reinstated his debt. This debt was enforced by "tormentors" who had legal grounds to torture him until the debt was paid in full.

THE KEY TO EXPERIENCING FREEDOM IS TO RELEASE THE OFFENSE, NO MATTER HOW JUSTIFIED IT SEEMS. YOU MUST MAKE THE CONSCIOUS DECISION THAT YOU WILL NO LONGER LIVE UNDER THE BONDAGE OF THE ENEMY.

Millions of Christians are being tormented by debt collectors because they are operating in bitterness and unforgiveness or because they have refused to break agreements with demonic powers. Every human being on planet earth owed a debt to God because of Adam's transgression. The consequence of this debt was death (both spiritually and physically). Whenever we refuse to forgive those who have trespassed against us, it is as if we are negating the efficacy of the cross and asserting that Jesus's blood was not enough. By doing this, we are operating according to the law rather than according to grace. Like the wicked servant, we run the risk of rejecting the unmerited favor of our Master and opting for living according to legalism. When we operate under legalism, the spiritual law of reciprocity is in full effect, and demons have legal grounds to collect the debt that was owed.

FEAR

Another means that demonic spirits use to enter our lives is the threshold of fear. I have often said that fear is the dinner bell for demonic powers. Just as rodents are attracted to food, demonic spirits are attracted to fear. Yet the Bible tells us,

> For God has not given us the spirit of fear; but of power, and of love, and of a sound mind. (2 Timothy 1:7)

The Greek word rendered "*fear*" in this verse is *deilia*, which means "timidity," "fearfulness," or "cowardice." Paul refers to fear as a "*spirit.*" It stands to reason that if fear is a spirit, it is not a spirit that originates from God because His "*perfect love casts out fear*" (1 John 4:18). Therefore, it must come from the devil. The spirit of fear is an evil spirit, and it can open the door to other familiar spirits as well. Imagine a doorman. A doorman's job is to open the door to guests who want to enter the building of an establishment. The spirit of fear is the doorman of the spiritual world. It opens the entrance to such demonic spirits as anxiety, depression, sickness, confusion, calamity, and death.

Any type of fear can produce bondage. When we rid our lives of the spirit of fear, we fire the doorman that grants access to demonic powers. For example, in my experience as a pastor counseling those who are ill, I have found that once you remove the fear of sickness, it becomes easier to get rid of the sickness itself. Similarly, once you eliminate the fear of rejection, it is easier to get rid of the spirit of rejection. The same is true for other types of oppression.

How do we overcome the spirit of fear? We must first receive the revelation that fear is the antithesis of faith. It distorts our perception of reality and paralyzes us. Let's look at these Scriptures that apply to faith and fear:

> *Thus says the* Lord; *cursed be the man that trusts in man, and makes flesh his arm, and whose heart departs from the* Lord.
> (Jeremiah 17:5)

> *Behold, his soul which is lifted up is not upright in him: but the just shall live by his faith.* (Habakkuk 2:4)

> *Now the just shall live by faith: but if any man draw back, My soul shall have no pleasure in him.* (Hebrews 10:38)

Faith overcomes fear because the eternal One in whom we trust is greater than all our fears. Faith is based on the truth, while fear is based on a lie. Both fear and faith originate from what we hear, so if we change the narrative, we will change the outcome. We need to saturate our minds and hearts with God's Word and trust Him to be faithful to that Word.

> *For you have not received the spirit of bondage again to fear; but you have received the Spirit of adoption, whereby we cry, Abba, Father.*
> (Romans 8:15)

For whatsoever is born of God overcomes the world: and this is the victory that overcomes the world, even our faith.   (1 John 5:4)

Since fear can hold such a grip on people, becoming a demonic portal, I ask you to take a moment right now to pray to be liberated from the spirit of fear:

Father, in the name of Jesus, I take authority over the spirit of fear in my life. I apply the blood of Jesus to my conscious and unconscious mind and declare that I have the mind of Christ. Fear has no place in either my heart or my mind; therefore, I deny access to every demonic spirit that seeks to gain entrance through fear. I exercise my authority in Christ and evict every demon and familiar spirit connected to fear, in the name of Jesus! Amen.

FAITH OVERCOMES FEAR BECAUSE THE ETERNAL ONE IN WHOM WE TRUST IS GREATER THAN ALL OUR FEARS.

NEGATIVE THOUGHTS AND MEDITATIONS

We must continually be watchful over our thoughts and meditations, whether they center on fear or any other negative emotion or idea. I have often said that "your meditation is your medication." In Scripture, the word *meditation* has a much different connotation than its modern application in many circles today (including new age groups), such as repeating a mantra. Just before Joshua led the Israelites into the promised land, the Lord said to him,

This book of the law shall not depart out of your mouth but you shall meditate therein day and night, that you may observe to do according to all that is written therein: for then you shall make your way prosperous, and then you shall have good success.   (Joshua 1:8)

In this verse, the Hebrew word translated *"meditate"* is *hagah*, which means "to moan or mutter (as in under the breath)." This ancient Hebrew practice was used to recite the Torah. It was a powerful tool for Scripture memorization. Unfortunately, many people do not realize the enemy's insidious attempts to hijack their lives through their thoughts and meditations and keep them from focusing on God's Word.

This is how it works: Satan sends thoughts to people, who then allow these thoughts to become a meditation; they speak them over and over again until the words come into manifestation. For example, a woman who has had a miscarriage but is now pregnant again may receive the thought, "This next child will be miscarried or stillborn!" She continues to entertain that thought, and she may begin speaking the idea. This process can open the door to a spirit of miscarriage and eventually lead to a physical miscarriage of the unborn child. Then, well-meaning believers surround her and assure her that God "took" her child. However, the truth is that the accuser took her child.

A precious friend of our family suffered multiple miscarriages, and, as a result, she experienced depression. She was taught and believed that God was the one causing her to have the miscarriages. It reached a point where she didn't even want to become pregnant again. One day, while speaking to her, I told her that it was not God's will for her to have these miscarriages. I showed her this passage of Scripture:

> And you shall serve the LORD your God, and He shall bless your bread, and your water; and I will take sickness away from the midst of you. There shall nothing cast their young [miscarry], nor be barren, in your land: the number of your days I will fulfill.   (Exodus 23:25–26)

This woman was shocked! She had no idea that it was Satan taking her unborn babies. Sometimes we unknowingly espouse false (and in certain cases, demonic) doctrines that affect our ability to operate in kingdom authority. Here is another example: many people do not believe they are forgiven by God because they have embraced a legalistic message of religion posing as the gospel of Jesus Christ. The Scriptures teach us that we are justified by grace and faith alone. (See Ephesians 2:8–9.) But the accuser of the brethren capitalizes on the ignorance and fear of believers through this false doctrine by getting them to believe that the difficulties they are going through are the result of their past sins. Indeed, there are natural and spiritual consequences to sin; however, when we believe a lie about the efficacy of the sacrifice of Jesus on our behalf, we can unwittingly open the door to familiar spirits.

Remember, the devil is the "father of lies." (See John 8:44.) If your theology is based on defeat or despair, you run the risk of releasing curses out of your mouth that invite and embolden demonic powers. (I discuss this process in more detail in coming chapters.) Beloved, we must give the enemy no place. Sometimes doing so can be much more insidious than we realize. Maybe you have been taught that it is not God's will to heal or that He uses sickness to teach us a lesson. Or perhaps you have formed the impression that God is a God of constant punishment or judgment. My friends, these are lies! Jesus came to give us life more abundantly. (See John 10:10.) Hallelujah!

DECEPTION

A portal that the enemy uses to gain access to our lives that is related to the door of negative thoughts and meditations is the doorway of deception. The apostle Paul wrote in 1 Timothy 4:1:

> Now the Spirit speaks expressly, that in the latter times some shall depart from the faith, giving heed to seducing spirits, and doctrines of devils.

The demonic doctrines that Paul is referring to are quite pervasive today. Countless times, I have had to confront such doctrines in my life and in the lives of others. This is why I often recommend that people who have come out of cults or false religions go through a process of spiritual deliverance. I remember one instance in which a woman had left Mormonism. This religion teaches that Jesus is the brother of Lucifer and that God has several wives all over the universe. Talk about crazy doctrines! Yet this woman would often insist that she had experienced more love in Mormonism than she now did in Christianity. I can't speak to that, but I do know that she refused to let go of her fantastical view of the demonic practices she had formerly engaged in. Consequently, she was greatly oppressed by demonic powers. She would constantly complain of health problems and other physical and emotional attacks. Through her own profession, she had given legal rights to the enemy.

In Romans 7:11, Paul wrote,

For sin, taking occasion by the commandment, deceived me, and by it slew me.

The Greek word translated *"deceived"* in this verse is *exapataō*, which means "to *seduce wholly*," "to beguile," or "to deceive." One of the dictionary definitions of "to deceive" is "deliberately causing (someone) to believe something that is not true, especially for personal gain."[12]

The accuser uses lies as a spiritual portal that grants familiar spirits legal access to torment and oppress believers. As the father of lies, the devil's goal is to get people to believe something that is not true. Every area of demonic bondage in a believer's life is connected to a lie they have embraced about God, themselves, or others. This lie blinds them to the truth of God's Word and causes them to deviate from His plan for their lives.

For example, many people were told that they would become just like a family member, in a negative sense. Once a person comes into agreement with a negative confession or word curse spoken over their life, they open the door to a spirit of deception. This, in turn, opens the portal to familiar spirits who seek to use the agreement with that lie as a basis to execute their malevolent agenda. But remember, demons have no power until we buy into their lie.

Another example is that many believers have embraced lies about the church. What do I mean by this? I am glad you asked! They may have a disapproving view of the body of Christ, often as the result of a negative experience they had in a local congregation or negative sentiments that were shared with them by other religious people. You will often hear individuals saying things like, "There is no love in the church!" or "The church is full of hypocrites!" This blanket statement is a lie that opens the door for them to be deceived and embrace familiar spirits, such as offense, false doctrines, and delusion, to name a few.

---

12. Lexico.com, s.v. "deceive," https://www.lexico.com/definition/deceive.

EVERY AREA OF BONDAGE IN A BELIEVER'S LIFE IS CONNECTED TO A LIE THEY HAVE BELIEVED ABOUT GOD, THEMSELVES, OR OTHERS.

Spirits of deception convince their victims to believe the insidious lie that the church is separate from the "kingdom," so they espouse a doctrine that suggests, "It's not about the church; it's about the kingdom of God!" They come to believe they do not need the "church" or "community" because they "hear from God for themselves." When this happens, people typically lose their joy in the Lord and gradually experience a decline in spiritual authority and power. This often leads them to loneliness, confusion, and demonic torment.

The key to being set free from such satanic tormentors is to come out of agreement with the lies of the enemy and to close the demonic portal by embracing a biblical doctrine about the church *and* the kingdom of God. I want to clarify that while it is true that a person can attend church and be involved in religious activities and still be distant from God, the notion that God promotes an attitude of disdain for His church is contrary to Scripture and diabolical. No sincere husband would endorse someone speaking negatively about his wife; the church is the bride of Christ, and even with all the flaws of the people within it, Jesus thought the church was "to die for"!

Jesus said, *"If you continue in My word, then are you My disciples indeed; and you shall know the truth, and the truth shall make you free"* (John 8:31–32). The key to freedom is a knowledge of the truth. Notice that Jesus did not say, "And you shall 'hear about' the truth, and it shall set you free." It is not the truth alone that you *hear* but rather the truth that you *know* in your heart that makes you free. Lies and deceit enslave us. But when we become intimately and experientially acquainted with the truth, we are liberated from the power of lies. The key to living a life of freedom is to reject the lies of the enemy and embrace God's truth.

In the next chapter, we continue our exploration of demonic portals as we examine openings related to curses and soul ties.

PRAYER OF RELEASE

Father, in the name of Your Son, Jesus, I come to You humbly and ask You to forgive me for any and every way in which I have compromised my walk with You, opening demonic portals to my life, including those of offense, fear, negative thoughts and meditations, and deception. I ask for the help of the Holy Spirit in renewing all negative patterns of thinking that have caused me to walk outside Your blessings. I pray against any forms of deception that I have come under, and I stand against any future deception. I also ask You to help me see the body of Christ as You see it. Help me to pursue Your Word, and Your Word alone, as my ultimate truth. On behalf of myself and my family, I declare, according to Isaiah 54:17, that *"no weapon that is formed against* [me] *shall prosper; and every tongue that shall rise against* [me] *in judgment* [I] *shall condemn."* From this day forward, I walk in the righteousness and truth of the living Word of God—Jesus, my Lord and Savior! Amen!

INSIGHTS FOR OVERCOMING

1. Offense or unforgiveness may be the single greatest doorway to demonization and oppression.

2. Faith overcomes fear because the eternal One in whom we trust is greater than all our fears.

3. We must be watchful over our thoughts and meditations, whether they center on fear or any other negative emotion or idea. "Your meditation is your medication."

4. Every area of demonic bondage in a believer's life is connected to a lie they have embraced about God, themselves, or others. This lie blinds them to the truth of God's Word and causes them to deviate from His plan for their lives.

PRACTICUM

1. Write down an offense someone committed against you that is still weighing on you right now. How has holding on to this offense affected your life? Surrender that offense to God and ask Him to enable you to completely forgive the offender and move forward with your life. Write a personal prayer of surrender and release next to the offense you listed.

2. What is your greatest fear at this moment? Look up Scripture verses that will build your faith in God as your Provider and Sustainer in all things. Out loud, express praise to God and tell Him that you trust Him to overcome all your fears.

3. Can you identify an area of your life in which you have accepted a lie as the truth or been deceived? What truths from God's Word counteract that lie or deception? Write down your thoughts about this. If you can't think of any lies you have embraced, ask the Holy Spirit to reveal if you have unknowingly accepted a demonic lie or fallen into deception in any way.

5

DEMONIC PORTALS: CURSES AND SOUL TIES

"Be not deceived; God is not mocked: for whatsoever a man sows, that shall he also reap."
—Galatians 6:7

Let us now continue to identify portals the enemy uses to gain entrance to our lives for the purpose of oppressing us and restricting our work in God's kingdom. In this chapter, we will discuss openings that have to do with the negative words we speak and the attachments and alliances we make.

EVIL COMMUNICATIONS

The influence of our communications, especially the words we speak, is so significant that I devote an entire chapter to it later in this book, entitled "The Power of the Spoken Word." In this section, we will look at how evil communications become an open door to the enemy's attacks.

> *Be not deceived: evil communications* [or companions] *corrupt good manners* ["*character*" NLT].   (1 Corinthians 15:33)

The Scriptures tell us that *"evil communications corrupt good manners,"* or good character. The phrase *"evil communications"* comes from two Greek terms. The first is *kakos*, which is derived from a root word meaning, among other things, "wicked," "troublesome," or "injurious." The second term is *homilia*, which signifies "companionship," "intercourse," or "communion." *Homilia* is the origin of our English word *homily*, "a religious discourse which is intended primarily for spiritual edification rather than doctrinal instruction."[13]

Essentially, Paul was informing the church at Corinth not to be deceived by evil discourse or conversation and that evil communication can bring corruption. The word *"corrupt"* here is translated from the Greek word *phtheirō*, which means "to corrupt" or "to destroy." This word has a connotation within the ancient Jewish religion of defiling or desecrating the temple.[14]

In other words, evil communications can defile or pollute our spiritual lives. What kind of conversations do you participate in? Have you ever gone away from a conversation feeling unclean? Such a feeling is due to the fact that negative words can be very powerful.

In my book *Unmasking the Accuser*, I share a story about a vision the Lord once gave me. In this vision, I saw two Christians having a conversation in the parking lot of a local church. As I looked closer, I noticed that there were two small demons on each of their shoulders. As these church members continued conversing, the demons would whisper gossip in each of their ears. Then, the two church members would begin to speak what the demons were whispering to them. As they did this, the demons would vomit on each of them. I asked the Lord what this vision meant, and He said, "The vomit was slander and gossip." He also said that "this slander and gossip is the sewage of hell."

Gossip is one of many access points through which we can experience spiritual contamination by the words we speak and the conversations we entertain. We need to recognize that conversations can edify, but they can also defile! One of the greatest misconceptions in the church is that "if it's just a conversation, it won't hurt anyone." Nothing could be further from the truth. Discussions can be dangerous. They have the ability to plant seeds that will later produce a harvest. We must vigilantly guard our ear

---

13. Lexico.com, s.v. "homily," https://www.lexico.com/definition/homily.
14. See *Strong's*, G5351, https://www.biblestudytools.com/lexicons/greek/kjv/phtheiro.html.

gates, hearts, and minds against spiritual contamination. Let us guard our gates!

> **WE MUST VIGILANTLY GUARD OUR EAR GATES, HEARTS, AND MINDS AGAINST SPIRITUAL CONTAMINATION.**

WITCHCRAFT AND THE OCCULT

Another portal through which familiar spirits enter into believers' lives is the doorway of witchcraft and the occult. It is essential to recognize that witchcraft is specifically prohibited by God. For example, the Lord told the Israelites in His commandments, *"You shall not allow a witch to live"* (Exodus 22:18). Why does God express such hatred toward witchcraft? Why did He require such severe punishment for those practicing witchcraft in the Old Testament?

We must understand that witchcraft was introduced to the human race by Satan. The apostle Paul wrote,

> *But I fear, lest by any means, as the serpent beguiled Eve through his subtilty, so your minds should be corrupted from the simplicity that is in Christ.*   (2 Corinthians 11:3)

Paul uses the word *"beguiled"* in reference to the exchange between Eve and the serpent in Genesis 3. The Greek word means "deceived," but it has a far more complex implication in the context of Scripture. First of all, the word *"serpent"* in the book of Genesis is an idiom for sorcery and divination. The Hebrew root word, *nāhaš*, actually means "to practice divination." We could say that the serpent brought Eve under a witchcraft spell. Notice what she says when confronted by God:

> *And the LORD God said to the woman, What is this that you have done? And the woman said, The serpent beguiled me, and I did eat.*
> (Genesis 3:13)

Eve essentially says that she was seduced or bewitched into eating the fruit from the Tree of Knowledge of Good and Evil. This was humankind's first encounter with "the unknown." Satan exploited Eve's curiosity of the unknown to manipulate and control her and to ultimately rob human beings of their spiritual authority. The word *occult* is defined by the dictionary as "supernatural, mystical, or magical beliefs, practices, or phenomena." It comes from the Latin word *occultare*, which denotes "hidden," "secret" or "concealed." [15] Notice that Satan seduced Eve with the proposition of gaining hidden or secret knowledge that she did not possess (which was a lie).

Just as Eve was corrupted in her mind by the beguilement of the serpent to the extent that her perspective was altered and she willfully consented to disobedience, those who practice witchcraft are under the bewitchment of the devil. They may be driven by a desire to know information that they believe God has concealed from them, or something they think He has denied them. This attitude is rooted in rebellion (unbelief) against God. Satan is a rebel, and those who practice witchcraft are behaving just like him.

> *For rebellion is as the sin of witchcraft, and stubbornness is as iniquity and idolatry.* (1 Samuel 15:23)

The Bible tells us that rebellion is witchcraft and witchcraft is rebellion. When people participate in witchcraft, whether knowingly or unknowingly, they are violating God's spiritual laws and essentially inviting demonic spirits to operate in their lives. Witchcraft brings spiritual corruption and pollution. The purpose of this section is not to make you superstitious but to highlight the importance of guarding your heart and life against malevolent and insidious forces that seek to hinder you spiritually. Anything you need to know in this life or the next should come from God. You must not consult horoscopes or chakras to gain earthly or spiritual knowledge; this is occult, or illegal, knowledge.

Moreover, any attempt to manipulate or control another person's will is a form of witchcraft as well. Avoid occult practices that invite familiar spirits into your life and home. Such practices include:

---

15. Lexico.com, s.v. "occult," https://www.lexico.com/en/definition/occult.

+ Divination

+ Ancestral worship

+ Santería

+ Juju

+ Obia

+ Black magic

+ White magic

+ Illusionism

+ Voodoo

+ Horoscopes

+ Crystals

+ Psychics

+ Mediums

+ Energy healing

+ Reiki

+ Yoga

+ Praying to or communicating with the dead (necromancy)

+ Chanting

+ The power of positive thinking/law of attraction

+ Spirit guides

+ Charms, spells, or enchantments

+ Demonic films or artifacts

+ Reading tea leaves

While this is not an exhaustive list, it can help give you an idea of certain things to avoid. Ask the Holy Spirit to give you guidance as to what specific things should be prohibited in your life. Stay away from any practice that does not point to Jesus as the only legal entrance into the supernatural.

ANY ATTEMPT TO MANIPULATE OR CONTROL ANOTHER PERSON'S WILL IS A FORM OF WITCHCRAFT.

GENERATIONAL CURSES

Another demonic portal we must be alert to is the entranceway of generational curses. The Lord told the Israelites:

> You shall not make to you any graven image, or any likeness of any thing that is in heaven above, or that is in the earth beneath, or that is in the water under the earth: you shall not bow down yourself to them, nor serve them: for I the LORD your God am a jealous God, visiting the iniquity of the fathers upon the children to the third and fourth generation of them that hate Me. (Exodus 20:4–5)

God warned His people that idolatry would open them to what is often called a "generational curse." Iniquity or trespass—a violation of a spiritual law—allows the legal ground for a curse to be established. In the above passage, the Hebrew word translated *"visiting"* in the phrase *"visiting the iniquity"* is *pāqad*, which signifies, among other meanings, "to pay attention to," "to attend to," "to lay upon as a charge," or "to be called to account." God was telling the Israelites of old that if they engaged in idolatry, He would hold the next generations accountable for their ancestors' iniquities.

However, in the book of Ezekiel, we see a prophetic word that is very important to note for this discussion because it points to a New Testament reality:

> The soul that sins, it shall die. The son shall not bear the iniquity of the father, neither shall the father bear the iniquity of the son: the righteousness of the righteous shall be upon him, and the wickedness of the wicked shall be upon him. (Ezekiel 18:20)

The Bible is telling us that, because of Jesus's work on the cross, children no longer need to bear the iniquities of their fathers. Each individual is responsible and accountable for their own sins. Christ has provided a way for forgiveness of our individual sins and for cleansing of generational curses.

I think one of the most interesting stories in the Bible is the account of Queen Esther and her uncle Mordecai. Essentially, this is a story about the preservation of the Jewish people in the Persian Empire through the courage of a young Jewish girl and the wisdom of her mentor Mordecai. However, there is much more to this story: this narrative actually gives us great insight into the way familiar spirits and generational curses operate.

After these things did king Ahasuerus [also called Xerxes] promote Haman the son of Hammedatha the Agagite, and advanced him, and set his seat above all the princes that were with him. And all the king's servants, that were in the king's gate, bowed, and reverenced Haman: for the king had so commanded concerning him. But Mordecai bowed not, nor did him reverence. Then the king's servants, which were in the king's gate, said to Mordecai, Why transgresses you the king's commandment? Now it came to pass, when they spoke daily to him, and he hearkened not to them, that they told Haman, to see whether Mordecai's matters would stand: for he had told them that he was a Jew. And when Haman saw that Mordecai bowed not, nor did him reverence, then was Haman full of wrath. And he thought scorn to lay hands on Mordecai alone; for they had showed him the people of Mordecai: wherefore Haman sought to destroy all the Jews that were throughout the whole kingdom of Ahasuerus, even the people of Mordecai. In the first month, that is, the month Nisan, in the twelfth year of king Ahasuerus, they cast Pur, that is, the lot, before Haman from day to day, and from month to month, to the twelfth month, that is, the month Adar. And Haman said to king Ahasuerus, There is a certain people scattered abroad and dispersed among the people in all the provinces of your kingdom; and their laws are diverse from all people; neither keep they the king's laws: therefore it is not for the king's profit to allow them. If it please the king, let it be written that they may be destroyed: and I will pay ten thousand talents of silver to the hands of those that have the charge of the business, to bring it into the king's treasuries. And the king took his ring from his hand, and gave it to

> *Haman the son of Hammedatha the Agagite, the Jews' enemy.*
>
> (Esther 3:1–10)

The most important factor in this story is that Haman, the most powerful official in the Persian Empire, was an Agagite. Haman was a descendant of Agag. You may be asking, "Who is Agag, and why is this fact about Haman's lineage so important?" I'm glad you asked!

Agag was the king of the Amalekites during the reign of King Saul. At that time, God had instructed Saul to destroy all of the Amalekites, including King Agag, but Saul decided to spare the king instead. This single act of defiance and rebellion was much more serious than Saul could ever have imagined because it had transgenerational effects. As a result of his sin, Saul was rejected from being king. However, perhaps even worse, Agag was allowed to have a posterity. (See 1 Samuel 15:1–29.)

Fast forward many years later to when the children of Israel are living in exile in the Persian Empire under King Ahasuerus. Haman, a direct descendent of King Agag, had one of the most powerful positions in the world. He hated the Jewish people and sought to have them destroyed. His ancestor, Agag, had been an enemy of Israel who was on a satanic assignment to destroy the people (and the seed) through which the Messiah of Israel would come into the world. The familiar spirit in Haman's bloodline sought to carry out a demonic assignment that had been hindered in previous generations.

Notice that the single act that provoked this generational curse was Mordecai's refusal to bow to Haman. Beloved, whenever we refuse to bow to the devil, there will be retaliation. But take heart! Remember that the Scriptures say, *"Greater is He that is in you, than he that is in the world"* (1 John 4:4).

Ultimately, the children of Israel declared a national fast to humble themselves before the Lord and seek His help, and God supernaturally thwarted Haman's plans and preserved His people. The Jewish feast of Purim is celebrated to remember what God did for Israel during this time. Haman was actually hung by his own gallows, which he had intended for Mordecai. This incident was more than just an act of God's intervention; it was His exposure of a familiar spirit that was seeking to bring destruction to the next generation and stop His plan of redemption from coming to fruition.

Thus, King Agag had entered into a covenant with demonic powers to destroy Israel in his generation. This established a spiritual debt that was passed on through his bloodline so that Haman was operating in the same spirit as Agag. Spiritual debts and demonic liens will continue to be in force until they are collected or discharged. This is why Jesus had to become the sacrificial Lamb; He fulfilled the debt that was owed by the entire human race, and we can now be free of any generational curse. (See, for example, John 3:16–17.)

CHRIST HAS PROVIDED A WAY FOR FORGIVENESS OF OUR INDIVIDUAL SINS AND FOR CLEANSING OF GENERATIONAL CURSES.

In Christ, we are redeemed from generational curses because Jesus Himself became a curse for us and received the penalty of sin on our behalf: "*Christ has redeemed us from the curse of the law, being made a curse for us: for it is written, Cursed is every one that hangs on a tree*" (Galatians 3:13). This is good news! We no longer have to live under the penalty of the sins of our fathers and mothers or the generations that went before them. However, this only stands true for those who are *in Christ* and who appropriate their rights under the new covenant. God is not the only one who takes note of sins in the bloodline. The accuser of the brethren seeks to exploit unrepentant sin and iniquity to propagate demonic strongholds.

One of the best earthly examples of this spiritual concept is the Emancipation Proclamation:

President Abraham Lincoln issued the Emancipation Proclamation on January 1, 1863, as the nation approached its third year of a bloody civil war. The proclamation declared "that all persons held as slaves" within the rebellious states "are, and henceforward shall be free."[16]

The Emancipation Proclamation freed all slaves in the Confederate states but not all slaves in all states of the Union. Slaves in Texas were freed by the Emancipation Proclamation in 1863, but they were not aware of it (that knowledge had been withheld from them by their supposed masters). Yes! Ironically, there were still slaves in parts of the South who did not know about this proclamation and were still functioning as slaves until the Union army arrived, and they were informed of it. The liberation of the slaves in Texas on June 19, 1865, is recognized as "Juneteenth" and is celebrated as a national holiday in the United States today. Full freedom was granted for all slaves in the United States by the Thirteenth Amendment to the Constitution, which was ratified in December 1865.

The reason I referred to the Emancipation Proclamation is to point to the fact that it is very possible to be liberated from something and not know it, and to remain negatively impacted as a result. Have you ever wondered why so many believers who love the Lord are constantly sick in their bodies? Have you ever asked yourself why the children of well-meaning Christians are often battling the same issues as the children of worldly or non-Christian parents? One of the reasons this is happening is because of the influence of familiar spirits. Many believers have been redeemed from the curse, but they still unknowingly live under the implications of that curse. This is why so many people are dealing with spiritual, emotional, and physical bondages.

UNGODLY SOUL TIES AND TRANSFERENCE OF SPIRITS

Another way familiar spirits gain access to people's lives is through ungodly "soul ties" and alliances. Simply put, a soul tie is a bond involving the mind, will, and emotions of two individuals or a group of people. A soul tie is essentially a bond that takes place through intercourse, intimacy, and/or communion. There are good soul ties, as in the biblical example of Jonathan and David (see 1 Samuel 18:1) or the bond between a husband and wife in a marriage sanctioned by God. However, there are also negative

---

16. "The Emancipation Proclamation," National Archives, https://www.archives.gov/exhibits/featured-documents/emancipation-proclamation.

soul ties where the bond or covenant is not sanctioned or authorized by God. The Scriptures exhort us:

> And have no fellowship with the unfruitful works of darkness, but rather reprove them.   (Ephesians 5:11)

> Be you not unequally yoked together with unbelievers: for what fellowship has righteousness with unrighteousness? and what communion has light with darkness?   (2 Corinthians 6:14)

In this verse, we are admonished not to be unequally yoked with unbelievers. The verse goes on to say, "What fellowship has righteousness with unrighteousness? and what communion has light with darkness?" The word "fellowship" is translated from the Greek word metochē, which means "a sharing," "communion," or "fellowship." The Greek word rendered "communion" is koinōnia, which can mean "fellowship," "association," "community," "communion," "joint participation," or "intercourse."

When we fellowship with unrighteousness or commune with darkness, it has a detrimental effect on our spiritual lives and can create soul ties. The people we are in fellowship with can invite familiar spirits. That is why the Scriptures tell us not to be "unequally yoked" with the unbelieving and the ungodly. God told the Israelites not to intermarry or commune with pagan nations because it would open the door to idolatry and spiritual contamination.

There are certain people who have yielded to demonic powers who can potentially "suck the joy" out of you. We might call them "spiritual vampires." Have you ever ended a phone call with someone and felt drained? This can actually be a sign that you are in the company of someone influenced by a familiar spirit. In mythology, a vampire is a deceased person who draws from the blood and life force of living people. In their efforts to revive their own lives, the vampires inevitably destroy the lives of their victims.

Another analogy is that of a tick that infects a person with Lyme disease. In some instances, and in certain species of ticks that are infected with the bacterium *Borrelia burgdorferi*, there can be a transmission of this bacterium from tick to host, causing an infection. Symptoms can include fever, chills, headaches, muscle aches, swollen lymph nodes, and even worse conditions. Similarly, there are certain people harboring familiar spirits who inadvertently infect the people they latch on to. This is why we must be mindful to avoid codependent relationships that can open our lives to spiritual bondage. We must also be aware of the need for boundaries in relationships as well as in counseling scenarios.

I heard the testimony of an individual whose friend was always experiencing calamity, confusion, and overall negativity. This individual would often give his friend advice and hang out with him. One day, he gave the friend a ride to a sporting event because the friend did not own a vehicle. On the way home from the event, they got into a really bad car accident, and the vehicle was totaled. On the surface, this may seem like a coincidence; but, from a spiritual standpoint, the accident was not arbitrary. We must understand that our connections with people can grant the very spirits operating in their lives access to ours. The friend had a spirit of calamity and chaos working in their life, and, as a result, the familiar spirit was able to transfer from them to someone they were close to.

This is why, when you regularly commune with negative people, you may often find yourself harboring negative thoughts and attitudes. When you fellowship with immoral people, you may begin to be tempted by immoral thoughts or feel a pull toward immoral behavior. My father frequently quoted the saying "Birds of feather flock together." We must be aware that who we connect with, fellowship with, or marry is very important.

A biblical example of ungodly soul ties and affiliations is the account of Queen Jezebel, the pagan wife of Ahab, a king of Israel in the prophet Elijah's day. In the book of 1 Kings, we read about the union between Ahab and Jezebel:

> And it came to pass, **as if it had been a light thing** for him to walk in the sins of Jeroboam the son of Nebat, that he took as a wife Jezebel the daughter of Ethbaal king of the Zidonians, and went and served Baal, and worshiped him. (1 Kings 16:31)

The Bible tells us that Ahab walked in the sins of his earlier predecessor Jeroboam, who encouraged idol worship; but to make matters worse,

Ahab married Jezebel. We can infer from the text that the act of marrying Jezebel was, in itself, a sin against God. Why? It says right there in the same verse that *"he took as a wife Jezebel the daughter of Ethbaal king of the Zidonians."* Jezebel was the daughter of the king of Zidon, whose name literally means "with Baal" or "under the favor of Baal." The Israelites were forbidden to intermarry with pagan nations. Not only was Ethbaal a pagan king, but he was also a priest of Baal, the Phoenician god of fertility and harvest. Baal was often referred to as "the lord of the harvest" or "the lord of thunder."

The marriage between Ahab and Jezebel was a demonic arrangement by familiar spirits to give the spirit of Baal legal rights to erect idolatrous altars in Israel. This disastrous situation is further expressed in the original language of the text in Jezebel's very name, one of the meanings of which is "Baal is husband to." Thus, Ahab did not just marry Jezebel, but he actually entered into a covenant marriage with the spirit of Baal itself. Consequently, as king of Israel, he brought the entire nation into a covenant with Baal!

WHO YOU CONNECT WITH, FELLOWSHIP WITH, OR MARRY IS VERY IMPORTANT.

The name Jezebel can also mean "unchaste," and Jezebel indeed operated in manipulation, seduction, intimidation, and control. Even though Ahab was the king, Jezebel was the one "calling the shots."

King Ahab's sin brought a curse upon the nation of Israel, and Elijah confronted Ahab about this wickedness:

And Elijah the Tishbite, who was of the inhabitants of Gilead, said to Ahab, As the LORD God of Israel lives, before whom I stand, there shall not be dew nor rain these years, but according to my word.

(1 Kings 17:1)

Elijah's confrontation with King Ahab was actually a confrontation with the spirit of Baal. The prophet spoke a decree over the heavens (and the demonic spirits operating in the atmosphere) preventing rain or dew from touching the entire nation. Why? Israel had turned to Baal as their god and looked to Baal for the dew of heaven. The drought was a judgment from God.

Although Jezebel was a historical figure, the "spirit of Jezebel" is a familiar spirit that inhabits and influences people even today. Like the original Jezebel, the spirit of Jezebel operates in idolatry, seduction, manipulation, and control. We see this spirit at work in the lives of women and men alike all over the world. Jesus told the church in Thyatira,

> *Notwithstanding I have a few things against you, because you permit that woman Jezebel, which calls herself a prophetess, to teach and to seduce my servants to commit fornication, and to eat things sacrificed to idols.*   (Revelation 2:20)

Why would Jesus make mention of a woman who had been dead for hundreds of years? He was not referencing the historical Queen Jezebel but rather to the *spirit* she represents. Notice that the rebuke was that they *"permit that woman Jezebel, which calls herself a prophetess, to teach and to seduce my servants to commit fornication, and to eat things sacrificed to idols."* When there is idolatry in any area of our lives, we become susceptible to the Jezebel spirit.

Often, the Jezebel spirit is generational in nature, passed down from mother to daughter, father to son, or even from aunts and uncles to nieces and nephews. Have you ever been under leadership that was domineering? Have you ever seen a woman who was manipulative and controlling? I want to be clear that not every woman who is strong and assertive is a "Jezebel." Many women have been wounded by the false accusation of having a Jezebel spirit. This is not a term we should throw around loosely. But any person who is bound by this domineering spirit is in need of serious deliverance and a radical encounter with the love of God.

We must be vigilant about legal claims in the spiritual realm that are perpetrated by spirits of darkness. We must be honest with ourselves about areas in our lives where we have come into agreement with the enemy concerning people, circumstances, and situations that are out of alignment with the Word of God. We are no longer under the law but under God's grace. Therefore, our debts are paid for by Christ through faith. We must come out of any agreements that are holding ourselves or others hostage to areas of spiritual debt, such as bitterness, manipulation, and control. We must *not* come into covenant with demonic forces that can infiltrate us, our homes, and our generational bloodlines. If we are currently in such a situation, Jesus Christ can restore us through His blood and substitutionary sacrifice.

I pray that these last two chapters have opened your eyes to demonic portals that you may have inadvertently opened in your life so that you can learn to close them and live in the freedom Christ has won for you.

PRAYER OF RELEASE

Father, in the name of Jesus, I thank You for the Word of God, which brings truth into my life. I thank You that Your Holy Spirit lives within me and brings to light those areas of my life that are in need of examining and cleansing. I pray that, from this day forward, I will desire to expose to You the places where I have allowed the enemy to gain a foothold so You can begin the cleansing and healing process. I take authority over any familiar spirits that I have given permission to enter my life, either under my own volition, out of ignorance, or through my family bloodline. I plead the blood of Jesus over myself and my household, and I thank You that Jesus's blood covers all of our iniquities. I also declare that my tongue will bless and not curse myself or others. I nullify any word curses in my bloodline that I have come into agreement with. I declare that those words have no effect on my life. I reject any deception I have given access to through rebellion or participation in witchcraft, the occult, or any other form of illegal access to knowledge. I recognize, according to Galatians 3:13, that Christ became a curse for me, and that my family and I do not need to walk under Satan's agenda but can fulfill Your assignment for our lives. I cancel all former patterns of destruction through curses, and I willingly submit myself and my family to the truth of Your

Word. I am blessed and not cursed because of the blood of Your Son. In Jesus's mighty name, amen!

INSIGHTS FOR OVERCOMING

1. Conversations have the ability to plant seeds that will later produce a harvest. We must vigilantly guard our ear gates, hearts, and minds against spiritual contamination.

2. When people participate in witchcraft, whether knowingly or unknowingly, they are violating God's spiritual laws and essentially inviting demonic spirits to operate in their lives.

3. Christ has provided a way of forgiveness for our individual sins and of cleansing for generational curses.

4. We must be honest with ourselves about areas in our lives where we have come into agreement with the enemy concerning people, circumstances, and situations that are out of alignment with the Word of God.

ASK YOURSELF

1. In what ways have I entertained or participated in evil communications? How will I resist the temptation to participate in evil communications in the future?

2. Is there any evidence of witchcraft and/or occult practices in my life or my family bloodline that need to be brought under God's authority and cleansing?

3. Who am I connected to or fellowshipping with that represents a liability to my spiritual journey with Christ?

6

HEALING THE WOUNDED SOUL

"Beloved, I wish above all things that you may prosper and be in
health, even as your soul prospers."
—3 John 1:2

We need to receive spiritual and emotional healing in order to defeat the enemy's attempts to gain access to our lives through the areas we discussed in the last two chapters, as well as other areas. For us to walk in the fullness of our freedom in Christ, we must be willing to surrender our wounded areas to the One who heals all wounds and restores our souls.

One of my favorite portions of Scripture is Psalm 23, written by King David. And one of my favorite parts of this psalm is the verse that says, *"He restores my soul: He leads me in the paths of righteousness for His name's sake"* (verse 3). Why is this verse such an important one in the Scriptures? David, the king of Israel, went through many devastating situations and circumstances. He was rejected by his elder brothers. He was anointed king at a very young age. He had a javelin thrown at him by his predecessor, King Saul. He was pursued by Saul for several years, and he had to flee for his life, sometimes hiding in caves. During his life, David was threatened by several assassination attempts, and he also faced the consequences of his participation in an adulterous affair and murder. Saying that King David had experienced trauma would be an understatement. He, of all people, knew the value of restoration. And Psalm 23 expresses that God our Shepherd restores souls.

Countless believers are suffering the debilitating effects of emotional trauma as they consciously or unconsciously experience affliction in their souls. But God is not just interested in your being healed in your physical body or renewed in your spirit; He is heavily vested in the condition of your soul. Third John 1:2 says, *"Beloved, I wish above all things that you may prosper and be in health, even as your soul prospers."* Notice that the writer of the text suggests that our lives will prosper to the extent that our souls prosper. What does this mean? The Greek word translated *"prosper"* and *"prospers"* in this verse is *euodoō*, which means "to grant a prosperous and expeditious journey" or "to lead by a direct and easy way."

Demonic spirits exploit the fragmented places in our souls so they can embed their nefarious activity there. I have heard it said that you will never find a "whole" person bound to sin and addiction. I believe this statement is true. God does not want us to be carted before the pearly gates in a wheelbarrow at the end of our lives and dumped out in pieces for the angels to sweep up. It is His will that we go through life whole rather than fragmented and broken. And, in this chapter, I want to teach you how to identify "soul wounds" and allow the power of God to restore you completely. Hallelujah!

IT IS GOD'S WILL THAT WE GO THROUGH OUR LIVES WHOLE RATHER THAN FRAGMENTED AND BROKEN.

SOUL WOUNDS

What is a soul wound, and how do we address such a wound? A soul wound is essentially any area in our mind, will, or emotions that has incurred damage from trauma, pain, or any other devastating event in life. A common source of a soul wound is rejection. When a person experiences rejection, they are under the impression that they are unwanted, unacceptable, unloved, and unworthy. Rejection is a very normal part of life; we will all experience some form of rejection in certain instances and at certain stages of our lives. We can use such instances to learn to trust in God, receive His love, and grow personally. However, when we internalize rejection, it becomes a soul wound.

If a soul wound is left untreated, it can actually develop a root system and become a bitter root through which familiar spirits can inhabit our lives. In the next few sections, I highlight common causes of soul wounds and describe their characteristics. This is not necessarily a complete list of soul wounds, but it is a guide that can help you identify and confront areas in your life where you have been emotionally wounded so that you can take these areas to the Lord and receive lasting freedom through the power of the Holy Spirit.

FATHER WOUNDS

I mentioned the fact that rejection is one of the primary sources of soul wounds, but there are different types of rejection, which cause different kinds of wounds. One wound that people frequently incur is what I call a "father wound." We see an example of this in the Bible in the relationship between King Saul and his son Jonathan.

> *Then Saul's anger was kindled against Jonathan, and he said to him, You son of the perverse rebellious woman, do not I know that you have chosen the son of Jesse to your own confusion* [shame], *and to the confusion of your mother's nakedness?* (1 Samuel 20:30)

Saul called his own son *"You son of the perverse rebellious woman."* That is probably not the best way to parent a young man. Saul was angry that Jonathan favored David, and he actually threw a javelin at his son. (See 1 Samuel 20:33). You may not have had a javelin thrown at you, but you may have had an emotionally absent or verbally abusive father. Perhaps you did not know your father while you were growing up (and possibly still don't know him), and you have felt the absence of a father figure in your life. Such experiences can inflict wounds in the soul, even if the wounding takes place subconsciously.

My father was present in our home, but he was often working and very seldom exhibited affection toward me. However, he was very proficient at discipline. I didn't know what it meant to hear the words "I love you" coming from a male figure. It wasn't until much later in life that I realized that I had been wounded emotionally by my father's lack of affirmation and affection. I do not say this to cast any aspersion on my father; he truly did the best he knew how to do. However, it is important for us to understand the underlying causes of the hurts and woundedness in our lives.

The following are some signs that you may be harboring a father wound:

+ Inability to submit to and trust authority (especially male authority)

+ Extreme stubbornness and/or self-will

+ Diminished capacity to discern a purpose and vision for one's life

+ Dysfunctional relationships with men

+ Strong tendency to rebel against God

+ Suspicion

+ Self-doubt

+ Insecurity

+ Identity confusion

+ Self-sabotage

> **A SOUL WOUND IS ESSENTIALLY ANY AREA IN OUR MIND, WILL, OR EMOTIONS THAT HAS INCURRED DAMAGE FROM TRAUMA, PAIN, OR ANY OTHER DEVASTATING EVENT IN LIFE.**

MOTHER WOUNDS

The role of a mother is key in developing a healthy atmosphere of nurturing, love, joy, and security in the home. If your mother was deeply wounded herself or operated with toxic emotions, you may have unknowingly incurred "mother wounds." Unlike father wounds, mother wounds can actually be inflicted in utero (while one is still in the womb). Just as a pregnant woman's placenta delivers vital nutrients to her baby, her emotional state and the trauma she has experienced in life can be transferred to her unborn child. This is why people are not always exaggerating when they say they were "born this way." Demonic spirits can afflict an unborn child with rejection, perversion, anger, and even addiction before that child is ever born.

In addition to this, many people were raised by controlling, manipulative, fearful, critical, and/or otherwise negative mothers. Instead of creating an atmosphere of nurturing and acceptance, these mothers fostered an atmosphere of chaos and rejection. The Bible says,

Every wise woman builds her house: but the foolish plucks it down with her hands. (Proverbs 14:1)

The Hebrew word translated *"builds"* is *bānâ*, whose meanings include "to establish" and "to cause to continue." The role of a wife and mother is to foster continuity in the home and in the children. But the Bible says that the foolish woman *"plucks [her house] down with her hands."* The Hebrew word rendered *"pluck down"* is *hāras*, among whose meanings are "to tear down" and "to destroy." This verse is profound. A woman has the power to build up her house (including her husband and children) or destroy her family.

Here are some signs that you may be harboring a mother wound:

- Manipulative and controlling
- Hypercritical and judgmental
- Inability to give and receive love
- Difficulty expressing emotions or showing affection
- Codependency, clinginess
- Misogyny (hatred or negative feelings toward women)
- Fear of abandonment
- Obsessive and compulsive behavior
- Sexual perversion and addiction
- Inability to maintain close relationships

SPIRITUAL ABUSE

There are various types of abuse, including physical, verbal, mental, financial, and others. Each of these types of abuse can cause trauma and soul wounds. However, for the purpose of this chapter, I am focusing on spiritual and emotional abuse. Why? Because the two most important parts of a person's being are their spirit and their soul.

I have prayed for and counseled thousands of people over the years who have been victims of someone who has abused their spiritual authority. In my book *Unmasking the Accuser*, I deal with a condition that I call PTSD (pastoral traumatic stress disorder). Just as many people have experienced post-traumatic stress disorder through exposure to severe trauma (including war, the tragic death of a loved one, or a natural disaster), there are countless people in the body of Christ who have experienced the devastation of spiritual and emotional abuse, often at the hands of an individual in spiritual leadership. Satan is the *accuser* of the brethren, but many leaders under demonic influence function as "*abusers* of the brethren."

The reason why emotional and spiritual abuse are so devastating is that people in spiritual authority represent God, and when these leaders abuse their authority, it is often very difficult for their victims to distinguish between the pain of the abuse and their personal relationship with the Lord. If you have suffered from spiritual abuse, I want you to truly understand this: God *did not abuse you, although those representing Him did*.

People who are the victims of spiritual abuse can experience soul wounds that are very difficult to overcome. Thankfully, the power of God is greater than the pain of abuse. Our heavenly Father is more than able to heal and restore us when we call upon Him with a heart of sincerity and humility. We may also need to seek help from a trusted Christian counselor.

I remember speaking to someone who had been the victim of extreme spiritual abuse. They had received false prophetic words from their pastor that convinced them to marry a person who happened to be a witch. They were constantly criticized, judged, and controlled by this pastor. They were even told that if they left the fellowship, they would become sick and die. Friends, this type of controlling behavior is demonic! If you find yourself under this kind of abusive leadership, I recommend that you leave immediately and seek counsel from a licensed counselor or other minister who is qualified to give insight in this area.

Another form of spiritual and emotional abuse is when those in church leadership use their influence and power to draw people to themselves rather than to God. This is a form of witchcraft. When people become more committed to their pastor than to Jesus Himself, this is a serious problem. Please do not get me wrong: I believe in honoring those in authority over us. However, when honor becomes worship, there is another spirit at work besides the Holy Spirit. We should all love our spiritual leaders and hold them in high esteem. We should even do our best to bless them as much as possible. But again, these things should be done as unto the Lord, according to Scripture; and doing so should draw us closer to God, not create dissonance and chaos in our spiritual lives.

Spiritual abuse can also be wielded in the form of mind games. Many Christians are literally losing their minds while sitting under certain leaders in the church who "gaslight" them (manipulate them psychologically) but then deny their words and behavior in a way that makes the people under them question their own sanity.

Here are some signs that you are under spiritual abuse:

+ Decreased ability to hear God's voice

+ Unproductive spiritual and emotional life

+ Fear of man

+ Constant spiritual and physical infirmity

+ Isolation from family members and friends

+ No longer able to make rational decisions

+ Constant strife and confusion in one's spiritual life

+ Regression in one's spiritual life

+ Calamity and devastation in one's life

+ Extreme financial lack and poverty

> **GOD IS MORE THAN ABLE TO HEAL AND RESTORE US WHEN WE CALL UPON HIM WITH A HEART OF SINCERITY AND HUMILITY.**

DEMONIC RESIDUE

Have you ever heard someone say that they had been through a difficult trial or season in their life, yet somehow they did not look like they had experienced such a trauma? They had received supernatural grace to see them through it, and it showed because of the joy and peace on their countenance; they had been spiritually strengthened even in the midst of their troubles. Then there are others who share testimonies of overcoming certain challenges or difficulties, but it often seems like there is something missing from the equation. Why? When it comes to the healing of a wounded soul, the question is not what a person has gone through but rather how much of what they went through is left behind as "residue."

The Bible says that the almighty God brought the Israelites out of Egypt *"with a mighty hand…and with signs, and with wonders"* (Deuteronomy 26:8). However, only about a year later, when Moses went up to Mount Sinai to receive the law of God, the Israelites compelled Aaron to make them a golden calf to worship, declaring, *"These be your gods, O Israel, which brought you up out of the land of Egypt"* (Exodus 32:4). Where did the Israelites get such a notion? It was the residue of Egypt! Even the gold that was used to forge the calf came from their time in Egypt. (See Exodus 12:35–36; 32:2–3.)

God is not merely interested in taking us out of Egypt; He wants to *get Egypt out of us.* Glory to God! Unfortunately, a false "grace" message has been perpetrated in the church, convincing people that because Jesus paid it all, there is nothing else for them to do in order to live in the freedom Christ won for them. Nothing could be further from the truth. The Bible says,

*Having therefore these promises, dearly beloved, **let us cleanse our-selves** from all filthiness of the flesh and spirit, **perfecting holiness** in the fear of God.* (2 Corinthians 7:1)

This verse describes what we often call "sanctification." The Greek word translated *"cleanse"* is *katharizō,* among whose meanings are "to remove by cleansing" and "to consecrate." Even though our spiritual being is born again according to 2 Corinthians 5:17, we must apply the Word of God and the power of the Holy Spirit to our souls (mind, will, and emotions) in order to appropriate the kingdom of God in our lives in its fullness.

The accuser of the brethren often attempts to convince people that they are not really born again because they find themselves struggling in a certain area of their lives or being demonically attacked. This is *not true.* Instead, many times, this means we are dealing with residue in our souls—for example, old thoughts, suggestions, and patterns. The dictionary defines the word *residue* as "a small amount of something that remains after the main part has gone or been taken or used."[17] I am not suggesting that there is a small amount of the sinful nature left in you that Jesus's blood did not cleanse you of when you were born again. Rather, I am saying that we often go through circumstances in our lives that have a tendency to leave behind a "residue" that must be addressed. In the Old Testament, God would often instruct the Israelites to wipe out the pagan inhabitants of the land so that there would be no residue of their presence that could come back to haunt them in the future.

Years ago, I went through a devastating season in ministry. Honestly, at the time, I did not think my ministry would survive. By the grace of God, I made it through that difficult time, but I was negligent to consider the *residue* that remained. Then the Lord asked me, "Son, did you pay attention to what was left behind?" Many pastors never get over an offense, a betrayal, or a church split because, long after the offender is gone, the spirit of offense that operated through them is still present. We must forgive and allow the fire of God to cleanse us from all hurt, disappointment, and bitterness that the enemy would attempt to operate through in the future. As I have said in other contexts, we must do as David did and "cut

---

17. Lexico.com, s.v. "residue," https://www.lexico.com/en/definition/residue.

off the head of Goliath" (see 1 Samuel 17:51) so that "giants" will not show up in future generations.

> **WHEN IT COMES TO THE HEALING OF A WOUNDED SOUL, THE QUESTION IS NOT WHAT A PERSON HAS GONE THROUGH BUT RATHER HOW MUCH OF WHAT THEY WENT THROUGH IS LEFT AS "RESIDUE."**

INNER HEALING

We must come to understand that our heavenly Father desires to speak to the wounded places in our lives and heal them with His all-encompassing love. Psalm 103:2–4 says:

> *Bless the LORD, O my soul, and forget not all His benefits: who forgives all your iniquities; who heals all your diseases; who redeems your life from destruction; who crowns you with lovingkindness and tender mercies.*

Years ago, I was in Liberia, West Africa, and I met a young lady during one of our village crusades who had been displaced by the civil war there. Her parents had been killed by a militia, and she was raised as an orphan in the jungle. She was a beautiful young lady, but she was emotionally disconnected and traumatized because of her experience. You could literally see the pain in her eyes. In one of the ministry sessions, I began to minister to her, and I walked her through a time of inner healing. I prayed to break the spirit of trauma off her life. She literally wept and wailed. This was the first time she had ever confronted her trauma, and she experienced healing. Glory to God!

Often, we are carrying wounds deep in our subconscious that we have never dealt with. The devil exploits these deep-seated wounds to manipulate our thinking and behavior in an attempt to bring bondage and affliction into our lives. I urge you again: give him no place! The power of the cross is efficacious in healing the wounded soul. As King David declared, *"He restores my soul"* (Psalm 23:3). The Shepherd of your soul is ready, able, and willing to deliver you and heal you of all your diseases, both spiritual and physical. In fact, He already healed you two thousand years ago by His death on the cross! It is time for you to walk in the fullness of Jesus's finished work and enjoy the life that He died and rose again to give you.

PRAYER OF RELEASE

Heavenly Father, I thank You for Your love and the sacrifice of Your Son, Jesus Christ. Your Word says in Romans 5:8 that *"while we were yet sinners, Christ died for us."* I thank You that because of Jesus's sacrifice, I can walk in spiritual victory. I therefore repent of harboring any and all pain, hurt, misunderstandings, grievances, and trauma from my past and my present. I choose to hold no one hostage for any of the soul wounds they have inflicted on me, because Christ's shed blood is sufficient for me. I ask You to forgive me for idolizing my wounds rather than seeking Your complete redemption of my life. Right now, as an act of my will, I choose to allow Your holy fire to cleanse me from all hurt, disappointment, and bitterness that the enemy would attempt to operate through today and in the future. I sever all ties to demonic residue from spiritual and emotional abuse, and I declare that from this day forward, I walk in complete healing from the inside out. In Jesus's mighty name, amen!

INSIGHTS FOR OVERCOMING

1. We need to receive healing spiritually and emotionally in order to defeat the enemy's attempts to gain access to our lives.

2. A soul wound is essentially any area in our mind, will, or emotions that has incurred damage from trauma, pain, or any other devastating event in life.

3. Some common soul wounds are "father wounds," "mother wounds," and spiritual abuse.

4. The Shepherd of your soul is ready, able, and willing to deliver and heal you of all your diseases, both spiritual and physical.

PRACTICUM

1. Identify areas of your life in which you have experienced trauma and/or soul wounds as defined in this chapter. Pray about each area, asking Jesus, the Good Shepherd, to bring healing and restoration to your soul.

2. Make a decision to forgive and release all those who have inflicted soul wounds on you, recognizing that you will need to rely on God's power and love to do this.

3. Think about someone in particular, whether a family member, friend, or colleague, who is hurting from a soul wound. In the Lord's leading, seek ways in which you can be an encouragement to that person, asking God to help you be an agent of His healing love.

7

THE POWER OF
THE SPOKEN WORD

*"Death and life are in the power of the tongue: and they that love it
shall eat the fruit thereof."*
—Proverbs 18:21

"Bless them which persecute you: bless, and curse not."
—Romans 12:14

The words we speak and the words we receive from others are so significant to our spiritual well-being that we need to carefully consider this area of our lives as we learn to overcome the influence of familiar spirits.

THE SPIRITUAL WORLD IS GOVERNED BY WORDS

The power of the tongue is a persistent theme in Scripture. When something is spoken into the atmosphere, it can change reality. Simply put, the spiritual realm is governed by words. The truth is, words can create or destroy. Yet, in my experience, nothing seems to be more understated in the church than the profound power of our words. So many Christians all over the world are unaware of the impact of what they say. As we will talk about further in the next chapter, the invisible world operates based upon the "law of permission." When we speak, we give permission or license to spiritual forces to operate. Our words set things in motion in the unseen realm that subsequently manifest in the natural world.

In case you might wonder if this process is a "new age" concept, I would like to bring your attention to Hebrews 11:3:

> *Through faith we understand that the worlds were framed by the word of God, so that things which are seen were not made of things which do appear.*

The world that we know was framed, established, and set into proper order by the spoken word of God. In keeping with this, when we speak God's Word, it literally changes our world. You must understand that new age "positive thinking" and "confession" are counterfeits of the confession and declaration taught in the Scriptures. As Christians, we are not inviting the "universe" or "positive energy" to assist us; we are actually using the spiritual authority that God has given us through His Word and by His Holy Spirit to bring about His will on earth. Jesus said,

> *And I will give you the keys of the Kingdom of Heaven. Whatever you forbid on earth will be forbidden in heaven, and whatever you permit on earth will be permitted in heaven.* (Matthew 16:19 NLT)

OUR WORDS SET THINGS IN MOTION IN THE UNSEEN REALM THAT SUBSEQUENTLY MANIFEST IN THE NATURAL WORLD.

WHAT WE SAY MATTERS

There is no denying that what we say matters. Our words affect us more powerfully than we often realize. And not only does what we say affect *us* greatly, but it also affects the people around us. This reality applies to both positive and negative words. The Scriptures tell us:

And the tongue is a fire, a world of iniquity: so is the tongue among our members, that it defiles the whole body, and sets on fire the course of nature; and it is set on fire of hell. For every kind of beasts, and of birds, and of serpents, and of things in the sea, is tamed, and has been tamed of mankind: but the tongue can no man tame; it is an unruly evil, full of deadly poison. Therewith bless we God, even the Father; and therewith curse we men, which are made after the similitude of God. Out of the same mouth proceeds blessing and cursing. My brethren, these things ought not so to be. Does a fountain send forth at the same place sweet water and bitter? Can the fig tree, my brethren, bear olive berries? either a vine, figs? so can no fountain both yield salt water and fresh. (James 3:6–12)

The Bible also says that *"death and life are in the power of the tongue"* (Proverbs 18:21). The Hebrew word translated *"power"* in this verse is *yād*, which literally means "hand." We could say that "death and life are in the *hand* of the tongue." Thus, another way of looking at this is to view the tongue as a demolition tool that can destroy or an instrument that can craft and construct.

THE MOUTH: A SPIRITUAL GATEKEEPER

Speaking blessings and declaring the promises of God can open doors of favor, increase, and prosperity in our lives. However, speaking what is contrary to the will of God can open the door to the influence and oppression of demonic powers. For example, spoken intently, statements such as "This headache is killing me!" can lead to infirmity and even a spirit of premature death.

What you proclaim, you permit! Are you *forbidding* demonic activity or *permitting* demonic activity with the words you speak?

Many people have unknowingly conceded rights to the devil and his demons in this way. Thus, one of the things we must fully recognize is the power of the tongue with regard to legal rights in the spiritual realm. We are responsible for protecting the spiritual jurisdiction that God has given us. Remember, the word *jurisdiction* is derived from the combination of two Latin words, *jur* (law) and *dictio* (saying), which we could interpret as meaning "the law of saying."

This is one of the most important spiritual principles the Lord has ever revealed to me. During a specific season in my life, I was going through unusual spiritual warfare, and I asked the Lord what door I had opened to the enemy. The answer I received should not have been shocking to me, although it was. The Lord said, "Your mouth is the open door!"

Jesus taught that we are responsible for what we say:

> *Every idle word that men shall speak, they shall give account thereof in the day of judgment. For by your words you shall be justified, and by your words you shall be condemned.* (Matthew 12:36–37)

I want to draw your attention to the sentence "*For by your words you shall be justified, and by your words you shall be condemned.*" The Greek word for "*justified*" is *dikaioō*, among whose meanings are "to render righteous or such he ought to be," or "to declare, pronounce, one to be just, righteous, or such as he ought to be." The word translated "*condemned*" is *katadikazō*, which means "to give judgment against (one), to pronounce guilty" or "to condemn." These are legal terms. Our words carry legal authority to bring either justification or condemnation. When the Lord spoke to me about my mouth being a gateway to experiencing unusual warfare, I was absolutely shocked because I realized that I was not being afflicted by some outside power. Instead, I had given legal rights to the enemy through the words I had said!

ARE YOU FORBIDDING *DEMONIC ACTIVITY OR* PERMITTING *DEMONIC ACTIVITY WITH THE WORDS YOU SPEAK?*

CURSES AND EVIL ASSIGNMENTS

Remember that iniquity or trespass (violation of a spiritual law) gives a curse legal grounds to be established. We talked about this in the account of Balaam. The prophet could not curse the Israelites because they were blessed by God. But then the Israelites entered into an ungodly, idolatrous agreement with the Moabites and experienced the effects of a curse, coming under the judgment of God. Curses include the spiritual consequences of sin. Adam and Eve were "cursed" after they violated God's law in the garden of Eden.

In Romans 12:14, the Bible tells us to refrain from cursing: *"Bless them which persecute you: bless, and curse not."* This is not a simple prohibition on profanity but is much deeper than that. The Greek word translated *"curse"* in Romans 12:14 is *kataraomai*, which literally means "to curse," "to doom," or "to imprecate evil upon." In Scripture, a curse often refers to an imprecation of evil, which means to speak ill or evil over or against someone. Clearly, the accuser of the brethren is in this line of business!

This is a very important spiritual principle. Familiar spirits use people's curses (again, words of imprecation spoken against others) to carry out their evil assignments. Too often, we assist them in these assignments. I have often said that *the tongue is a landing strip for the devil.*

Every day, millions of people inadvertently engage in "cursing" themselves or others without realizing the implications of their words in the spiritual realm. Allowing words to proceed from your mouth that are contrary to the will of God can open the door to demonic powers. As if the words that are spoken were not evil enough, any malicious intent behind the words is also potent. In the realm of the spirit, our words have weight.

This is why parents have to be careful what they say to their children. For instance, a mother may say to her son in a moment of frustration, "You can't do anything right!" Those words can set in motion spiritual forces that can affect that son in a negative way.

Once a curse is spoken and the recipient of the curse accepts it in some manner, the curse has power. This reality is based on the "law of agreement," which has both negative and positive applications. Remember what Jesus taught regarding the power of agreement in prayer:

> *Again I say to you, That if two of you shall agree on earth as touching any thing that they shall ask, it shall be done for them of My Father which is in heaven.* (Matthew 18:19)

Unfortunately, the power of agreement can also work in a destructive way. I vividly remember ministering to a young woman who told me that her former spiritual leader had spoken a word curse over her saying that she would have infirmity in her body. A "word curse" refers to an imprecation of evil spoken with spiritual authority. Because this woman was under the authority of the spiritual leader, the words the leader spoke had efficacy (especially considering that they were spoken under the guise of prophecy). After she left the ministry, she literally found a mass in her body. This type of situation happens all too often. Agreement is empowerment. The moment you come into agreement with someone (or something), you give that person (or thing) power. Every so-called prophecy is *not* from God! Our heavenly Father does not afflict people with cancer or any other disease. You must come out of agreement with any word curses that have been spoken over your life and begin declaring God's truth instead. You can confess, "I am healed in my body. I walk in divine health! I will live a long and fruitful life, in the name of Jesus!"

THE MOMENT YOU COME INTO AGREEMENT WITH SOMEONE (OR SOMETHING), YOU GIVE THAT PERSON (OR THING) POWER.

CURSES WITHOUT CAUSE

Proverbs 26:2 tells us, *"As the bird by wandering, as the swallow by flying, so the curse causeless shall not come."* To be effective, a curse must have a "cause," or a basis for being set in motion. The Hebrew word rendered *"causeless"* in the above verse is *hinnām*, among whose meanings are "freely," "for nothing," "without cause," "for no purpose," "in vain," and "undeservedly." If there is no opening for the curse, it has no power.

People have actually spoken curses over me, either in person, through written notes, or through email. But I reject every curse in the name of Jesus and send it back to the pit of hell. The Bible is abundantly clear that *"no weapon that is formed against you shall prosper; and every tongue that shall rise against you in judgment you shall condemn. This is the heritage of the servants of the* LORD, *and their righteousness is of Me, says the* LORD" (Isaiah 54:17).

As mentioned previously, in the ancient world, curses were verbal pronouncements or imprecations that were influenced by evil spirits and carried spiritual authority. These verbal pronouncements had the ability to orchestrate forces such as sickness, calamity, destruction, and/or even death. Yes! Words can create or destroy.

If the power of our words can release blessings or curses over our lives or the lives of others, then it is highly possible that many calamities that people experience are the result of negative words that have been spoken by them, to them, or over them. You will notice that certain times of the year often give rise to accidents and calamitous events. This may be a sign that word curses are being released into the atmosphere. We must recognize these devices and counter them with the blood of Jesus and the authority of His name.

RELEASE GOD'S BLESSINGS

Let us always seek to use our words to build up and not tear down. The Bible says, "*A man shall be satisfied with good by the fruit of his mouth: and the recompense of a man's hands shall be rendered to him*" (Proverbs 12:14).

When I first started my ministry, I was told that the city where we live, Tampa Bay, Florida, was a very difficult place to pastor. I would often hear people say things like, "This is hard ground!" Other people would refer to it as a "spiritual graveyard." These words were coming from pastors who had been given spiritual authority by God over the territories the Lord had called them to pastor, yet their words were negative and filled with defeat. No wonder it was so difficult to minister there! They (not the devil) had given spirits of oppression, bondage, and stagnation the legal right to lay siege on the spiritual atmosphere of the city. These spirits were tasked with bringing delay and discouragement to spiritual leaders.

The more I subscribed to this narrative, the more difficult it was for me to pastor and for my church to grow. Then, one day, the Lord revealed what I and so many other pastors had been doing to the spiritual fabric of our city. I began to declare that Tampa Bay was "The Bay of the Holy Spirit." This change in decree started to reshape and shift our church culture. We broke through, and our church began flourishing!

> *You shall also decree a thing, and it shall be established to you: and the light shall shine upon your ways.* (Job 22:28)

Through our Scripture-based words, God wants us to release blessings over our families, homes, churches, cities, and nations. As you pay attention to what you are speaking, and as you actively reject all word curses and statements that are contrary to God's Word, remember this truth:

> *Christ has redeemed us from the curse of the law, being made a curse for us: for it is written, Cursed is every one that hangs on a tree: that the blessing of Abraham might come on the Gentiles through Jesus Christ; that we might receive the promise of the Spirit through faith.* (Galatians 3:13–14)

PRAYER OF RELEASE

Heavenly Father, I acknowledge that You want my words to bring Your truth, love, and blessings to the world. I repent for all the times I have used my words for negative purposes—complaining about my circumstances, bringing an atmosphere of hopelessness and despair, or speaking ill of other people. I break any negative agreements I have made with the spiritual forces of darkness, and I ask You to forgive me and to cleanse me from all unrighteousness. Thank You that Christ has redeemed me from the curse of the law. Father, fill me anew with Your Holy Spirit, and may every word I speak reflect the fruit of Jesus's righteousness. Let there be no cause for any curse to have power in my life as I walk in Your ways. In Jesus's name, amen.

INSIGHTS FOR OVERCOMING

1. The spiritual realm is governed by words. When we speak, we give permission or license to spiritual forces to operate. Our words set

things in motion in the unseen realm that subsequently manifest in the natural world.

2. The Bible says that *"death and life are in the power of the tongue"* (Proverbs 18:21). What you proclaim, you permit.

3. Speaking blessings and declaring the promises of God can open doors of favor, increase, and prosperity in our lives.

4. Iniquity or trespass (violation of a spiritual law) gives a curse legal grounds to be established, but a curse without cause has no power.

ASK YOURSELF

1. What words do I regularly speak about the state of my life? Am I *forbidding* demonic activity or *permitting* demonic activity with these words?

2. What is the first thing I say when something goes wrong? If it is a negative statement, how can I change what I say to align with God's Word?

3. Is what I am saying to or about other people positive or negative? How can I speak to others in a way that uplifts and encourages them, ultimately pointing them to their loving and all-powerful heavenly Father?

8

THE LAW OF ATTRACTION

"Be you not unequally yoked together with unbelievers:
for what fellowship has righteousness with unrighteousness?
and what communion has light with darkness?"
—2 Corinthians 6:14

We talked previously about the power of spiritual meditation, which has profound implications for us as we read and reflect on the Word of God and allow it to renew our minds, change our negative and erroneous patterns of thinking, and conform us to the image of Jesus. However, we also discussed how the spiritual principle of meditation has been adopted (I would even dare say "hijacked") by the new age community and twisted into something far different from what God originally intended.

Many people all over the world are settling for a counterfeit version of faith. They go to conferences and motivational seminars to learn how to use the power of the mind to achieve success in their relationships, businesses, and careers. Most of this instruction seems very harmless, but it can be much more diabolical than people fathom: positive thinking, chanting, channeling, and visualizing are all methods taught at these seminars. These are also tools used in the practice of witchcraft.

I distinctly remember watching a session on the Internet from a very popular motivational speaker who told the audience members to lift their hands and "let the universe flow through them." The Lord revealed to me that the people in that auditorium (all fifteen thousand of them) were inviting familiar spirits into their lives. These familiar spirits would initially seem to bring blessings, but then they would begin to bring curses and destruction. This is the reason why you will find that many successful businesspeople who incorporate such practices to achieve success often end up with broken marriages, fractured families, and even failed health. Why? Because their success was accomplished through demonic powers.

The Bible tells us, *"The blessing of the LORD, it makes rich, and He adds no sorrow with it"* (Proverbs 10:22). God's blessings do not have curses attached to them. The enemy, on the other hand, always takes from people far more than he gives. This is why we must be very careful what spirits we invite and attract into our lives.

The new age approach to meditation is often referred to as the "law of attraction," which incorporates the concept of the power of our words. Let me be clear: the law of attraction is a spiritual principle, but perhaps not in the way you might think. The idea is that if you concentrate on certain things hard enough and speak about them into the atmosphere, your desires will materialize. This is a very popular philosophy that is even embraced in many Christian circles. Remember, the devil is a counterfeiter; he is not capable of any original ideas. As we noted earlier, while confession and declaration are biblical concepts, any attempt to manipulate the spiritual world or God Himself in order to fulfill your fleshly desires is not from God.

You may hear people say things like, "The universe blessed me with this house" or "The universe gave me this car." Beloved, the universe does not bless anyone! God is the source of all life and blessings. (See James 1:17.) Unfortunately, many people are inviting familiar spirits through these insidious new age practices. We discussed in the last chapter that, when we speak, we set spiritual forces in motion that can affect us for good or for evil. The question is, with our thoughts, meditations, and words, *what are we attracting?*

DEMONIC MAGNETIC ATTRACTIONS

The law of attraction operates in various ways. As we delve deeper into an understanding of how this law works, it is important for us to recognize that not all attraction is natural. The word *attraction* is variously defined as "the act, process, or power of attracting," "personal charm," "the action or power of drawing forth a response: an attractive quality," and "a force acting mutually between particles of matter, tending to draw them together, and resisting their separation."[18]

Every person on this planet experiences natural attraction to other people, places, and things. There may be a certain tone of voice, look, style, or hue that draws their attention. Such attraction is based on their personality, upbringing, and socialization. However, there is such a thing as demonic attractions. These are attractions that are facilitated by familiar spirits.

For example, a woman who has been abused in a relationship with her significant other may find herself drawn to the identical personality profile in different men who do not know each other. She may even move to another city or state and find herself getting into relationships with the same type of abusive man over and over again.

Here is another illustration: two people who have a past of sexual immorality will somehow locate each other in a large church. Even though this church may have thousands of members, they find themselves gravitating toward each other, and they soon meet. Though they are often unaware of it, the force attracting them to each other is a spirit of lust. For example, I heard a story from a pastor who was separately counseling a man and a woman who lived in different but nearby states. The man had been disciplined for being involved with women in his church in an inappropriate manner. The woman had been involved in multiple affairs with several different men and was seeking deliverance. This pastor told me that there was a regional conference in their area, and both of these individuals attended. Though they had never met each other before and there were hundreds of people in attendance, they were seen gravitating closer and closer to each other from across a large room. Eventually, they met at the coffee table and began talking. Ultimately, they exchanged numbers and "found themselves" on a date together. This type of scenario is very common.

The law of attraction operates in other types of associations as well. A friend of mine told me that he had been involved in a cult and hadn't

---

18. *Merriam-Webster.com Dictionary*, s.v. "attraction," https://www.merriam-webster.com/dictionary/attraction.

realized it. Eventually, he recognized that he had to leave for the sake of his spiritual well-being. Moreover, this wasn't the first time he had unknowingly joined a cult. The Lord later told him that the reason he kept being drawn to cults was that he had a spirit of deception operating in his life. When he repented to the Lord, confronted the spirit of deception, and renounced that demonic spirit, he was never a part of another cult again. Hallelujah!

> **WITH YOUR THOUGHTS, MEDITATIONS, AND WORDS, WHAT ARE YOUR ATTRACTING TO YOUR LIFE?**

INVOKING OCCULT POWERS

Sometimes, the law of attraction is manifested through the use of occult powers. If you are familiar with my ministry, you know that I have taught extensively on the dangers of witchcraft. We have discussed some of these dangers in previous chapters. Unfortunately, many Christians are unknowingly engaged in this occult behavior. There are many aspects to witchcraft, but the two we are focusing on in this book are (1) manipulation, control, and domination, and (2) employing the power of evil spirits. These two aspects are often connected.

Have you ever looked at a person and said, "I want to connect with them"? Many of us have said things like that either in our thoughts or out loud. There is actually nothing wrong with a desire to connect with someone, such as a potential friend, a pastor who speaks deeply to our spiritual state, or even a mentor. Yet such a desire becomes dangerous and sinful when people invoke occult powers to facilitate the connections they seek. For example, a man who wants to romantically connect with a woman in a church setting but uses spirituality as a veil to conceal his lustful desires is indeed invoking familiar spirits. Or a person pretending to connect with a ministry for spiritual purposes but actually seeking financial assistance as the only motive for the connection is also invoking familiar spirits.

There are even times when a woman or man will say to themselves about a particular person, "I will have them!"—regardless of whether that person is already married or in a committed relationship. Such thoughts and declarations can open the door to familiar spirits who imitate the voice of the Holy Spirit in order to "confirm" these evil desires as spiritual and justified. The individual desiring the relationship may be deceived by false dreams, visions, and spiritual encounters. Of course, I am not referring to our seeking the leading of the Holy Spirit, which draws us and connects us to people and places for God's purposes. I am talking about (knowingly or unknowingly) using ungodly spiritual forces to obtain connections that God has not sanctioned or to manifest evil desires.

Whether you are a new or seasoned believer, you may be wondering how to be certain you are hearing God's voice or how you can differentiate between the voice of the Holy Spirit and the voice of a demonic spirit. I understand that this is a serious question for many believers who find themselves in situations where they are uncertain about God's will. However, let the following be a guide to you: the Holy Spirit will always lead you into all truth. That is what the Scriptures teach us. (See John 16:13.) Therefore, you may be assured that the Holy Spirit would never lead or tempt you to engage in behavior that is contrary to God's Word.

Once, a woman came to me for prayer, telling me that God had shown her the man who was to be her husband—except that he was married to someone else. She said the Lord had revealed to her that his wife was going to die, and she and the man would be married. She insisted that God was leading her to pray for the wife's death. I told this woman in no uncertain terms that this idea had come from a demonic spirit and not the Holy Spirit. As ridiculous as this story may seem, it actually happened. There are many people in the body of Christ who are bound by such demonic spirits. If you realize that you have been deceived in a similar way, repent immediately and ask God to deliver you from the familiar spirit. There is freedom and healing in Christ.

THE HOLY SPIRIT WOULD NEVER LEAD OR TEMPT YOU TO ENGAGE IN BEHAVIOR THAT IS CONTRARY TO GOD'S WORD.

"RESIDUE" AND DEMONIC ATTRACTION

Like the woman in the previous story, many people are unaware of the activity of insidious familiar spirits working in their lives. I often tell people to take inventory of what is "pulling" or attracting them. This can help them recognize the presence of an evil spirit. Ask yourself the following: "What's pulling me?" "Who do I gravitate toward?" "What is a common characteristic of people in my circle?"

I have been a pastor for a number of years, and I have noticed that many people tend to gravitate toward others based on the spirit that is operating in them. For instance, I have noticed that when people are offended, they tend to gravitate toward other people in the church who are offended. If you pay very close attention, you will see that the offended individual never brings their initial grievance to some random person in the church. They always bring the offense to someone they believe shares the same sentiment.

Most of us will have at least some relationships with friends that are based on healthy interests. But we need to evaluate the full range of our relationships. For example, do you find yourself sometimes gravitating toward people who gossip? Or do you experience the same negative or abusive experiences at every church you attend? This could be an indicator that a familiar spirit is at work.

As we talked about in chapter 6, "Healing the Wounded Soul," sometimes there is a "residue" of hurts or negative attitudes left over in our lives because we have not completely surrendered our pasts to God or been fully healed emotionally. This residue can attract familiar spirits seeking an opportunity to legally enter our lives. Have you ever thought you were delivered from something, but then the issue reared its ugly head again? This doesn't mean that God didn't do a work in you, but it may mean that there is still more work to be done in certain areas of your soul.

I clearly remember a season in my life in which God delivered me from a spirit of lust. I was going through a time of great testing and temptation, being attacked in my mind with lustful thoughts. I went to God in prayer, and while I was saying a prayer of deliverance and breakthrough, it felt like a bird flew off of my head and went off into the distance. Something literally broke. I had experienced deliverance in that area before, but the

Holy Spirit was now doing a deeper work in my soul that would ultimately liberate me from the power of that spirit. Additionally, although I was supernaturally delivered from the influence of that demonic spirit, in order to maintain a pure mind, I needed—and still need—to make a conscious, daily decision to obey God's Word and *"flee youthful lusts"*:

Flee also youthful lusts: but follow righteousness, faith, charity, peace, with them that call on the Lord out of a pure heart.

(2 Timothy 2:22)

After we receive God's deliverance from a certain issue, even though we need to daily commit to following God's ways, we should not continue to experience a raging struggle with that issue every day. When this happens, it can mean that there is indeed some residue that needs to be addressed. If it is not dealt with, that residue can pull us toward sin and ultimately lead to deeper levels of bondage. This is why many leaders struggle in their walks with the Lord. They love God, but they need to do some spiritual housecleaning in order to address the various areas of sin and bondage in their lives. Contrary to popular belief, demons do not just "go away" with time; if we do not confront them, they actually become stronger. I believe that God is taking the church through a deeper level of cleansing and sanctification that will enable His people to function in His glory in the way He intends. For the next great move of the Spirit of God, we need *"clean hands, and a pure heart"* (Psalm 24:4).

We see the effects of such personal "residue" in the life of Moses. Moses fled Egypt because he had murdered a man in anger. (See Exodus 2:11–15.) Note that, years later, the same issue of anger kept him from entering the promised land. Moses became angry at the Israelites and struck the rock that God had only told him to speak to (an act that might seem to pale in comparison to murdering someone), and because of his disobedience, he was unable to enter into the land with the rest of the Israelites. Why? The same spirit had motivated both actions: it was a spirit of anger! Of course, Moses was operating under the old covenant; he was not born again, and he didn't have the Holy Spirit dwelling inside him. But we have the advantage of the cleansing blood of Jesus and the presence of the Holy Spirit as our Guide and Comforter to overcome any such residue in our lives.

If you are trapped in a cycle of sin or defeat, declare that the blood of Jesus breaks the power and the pull of that demonic spirit. We will talk more about applying the blood of Jesus to our lives for deliverance in chapter 11, "The Power of the Blood."

GOD'S LOVE: THE DEMON REPELLANT

Years ago, I was ministering overseas, and I had a very intense time of preaching. Afterward, the pastor of the host church brought two young ladies to me for prayer in the sanctuary. He asked me to pray for them to get married, as they were both well beyond what some would consider "marriageable age." As I was praying for one of the young women, the Lord told me that she had an ungodly soul tie. The moment I said (through the interpreter) that there was soul tie, this young lady immediately began manifesting a demonic spirit. Her eyes became bloodshot, and she began screaming in her language. She then proceeded to spit on the host pastor and his wife.

There were many demons inside this woman, and because I was familiar with deliverance, I began to cast out the evil spirits as they manifested. I proceeded to ask one of the spirits how it had been able to enter her. Before it could reply, the Holy Spirit revealed the answer to me, and I said, "It was through your grandmother!" The moment I revealed this truth, the young woman started to scream. But this scream was different. When I told the familiar spirit in her to leave, it began to say, "No, no, no!" It was almost a cry of desperation. Finally, a spiritual word of knowledge came to me, and I shared with the young lady, "God loves you unconditionally." She began weeping and saying that she could never be forgiven for the things she had done. I asked God to baptize her in His love, and I could see the grip of the spirit of perversion, confusion, and death being broken. Eventually, she was totally free. Glory to God!

This experience taught me a profound lesson about demons: they cannot stand the love of God! The agape love of God is like a repellent for powers of darkness. The Bible says, "*Charity [love] never fails: but whether there be prophecies, they shall fail; whether there be tongues, they shall cease; whether there be knowledge, it shall vanish away*" (1 Corinthians 13:8). The love of God is the most powerful force in the universe. When we walk in the unconditional, agape love of God, demonic powers lose their hold and strength. God's love can break through all satanic attachments. Hallelujah!

> **THE AGAPE LOVE OF GOD IS LIKE A REPELLENT FOR POWERS OF DARKNESS.**

THE POWER OF PERMISSION

In connection with the law of agreement, we should never underestimate the power of permission. The word *permission* is defined as "consent" or "authorization."[19] Throughout this book, we have talked about how familiar spirits are constantly seeking our agreement for them to operate in our lives. We must always be mindful of what we grant permission to because, again, whatever we permit, we authorize; and whatever we authorize, we empower.

God warned the Israelites not to make a covenant with the inhabitants of the land of Canaan, or it could become a *"snare"* to them:

> *Take heed to yourself, lest you make a covenant with the inhabitants of the land where you go, lest it be for a snare in the midst of you: but you shall destroy their altars, break their images, and cut down their groves: for you shall worship no other god: for the* LORD, *whose name is Jealous, is a jealous God: lest you make a covenant with the inhabitants of the land, and they go a whoring after their gods, and do sacrifice to their gods, and one call you, and you eat of his sacrifice; and you take of their daughters to your sons, and their daughters go a whoring after their gods, and make your sons go a whoring after their gods.*
> (Exodus 34:12–16)

As we consider this passage, let's review the relationship between spiritual permission and legal rights. For the Israelites' own protection, God admonished His people to refrain from unsanctioned covenants with

19. Lexico.com, s.v. "permission," https://www.lexico.com/en/definition/permission.

pagan nations. The Lord knew that these covenants could open demonic portals that would lead Israel into spiritual bondage. The same principle is true for us today. It is not enough for us to refrain from evil ourselves; we must also refrain from agreement with those who practice evil.

Can you imagine giving your friend a ride to a liquor store so they could rob it? And suppose this friend were caught. Would you be surprised if you were arrested along with them? Now picture yourself standing before the judge and asking, "Why am I being charged with robbery?" You would probably be scoffed at in the courtroom. Why? Because you were a willing accomplice and accessory to a crime. You did not commit the physical act, but you gave consent, permission, authorization, and support for the crime to be perpetrated.

Demons recognize the power of the permissions we grant. That is why they are constantly seeking to deceive believers into giving consent to their plans. Remember this: the devil cannot do anything in your life without your permission! Demons cannot come into your house without your authorization; this is why what you allow into your home is so important. Many believers are bringing in ungodly artifacts, objects, paintings, and other points of contact that invite evil spirits. Countless other Christians are watching pernicious images like pornographic films that bring familiar spirits into their home environments. It is sad to even think that many children are exposed to pornography in Christian homes. I do not say this to condemn anyone who may be struggling in these areas but to give deeper insight into places in your life that may be creating an atmosphere that is antithetical to the presence of God.

THE LAW OF ALTARS

Throughout the Bible, we see the law of altars, which has great significance with regard to the law of agreement. In the ancient world, altars were used to invoke the presence and power of spiritual beings. The building of altars to the Lord seemed to be intuitive to people in the Bible. For example, when Jacob had a supernatural visitation from God, he built an altar to the Lord to memorialize his divine encounter. (See Genesis 28:10–22.) In Genesis 15, God commanded Abraham to make an altar before entering into a covenant with him.

As we will discuss in more depth in chapter 10, "Renouncing Evil Covenants and Oaths," God is a God of covenants and altars. Yet the Israelites did not only build altars to honor and revere God. When they were rebellious, they often erected altars to invoke *"strange gods."* (See, for example, Deuteronomy 32:16; 1 Samuel 7:3.) It is important to understand that other gods do not exist; therefore, these *"strange gods"* were (and are) demons, including familiar spirits. Today, an altar is any place where we invite, invoke, and commune with spiritual powers.

An altar grants permission for a spiritual power to operate in a certain place or territory. If that power is evil, it needs to be cut off. In the Old Testament, when God dealt with His people concerning their participation in idolatry, He would command them to tear down and/or cleanse the altars. The kings of Israel who actively sought to obey the Lord removed pagan altars from the land, as we see in this example:

> *And Asa did that which was good and right in the eyes of the* Lord *his God: for he took away the altars of the strange gods, and the high places, and broke down the images, and cut down the groves: and commanded Judah to seek the* Lord *God of their fathers, and to do the law and the commandment.* (2 Chronicles 14:2–4)

The true power of any people is determined by the purity of their altar, a theme we will return to later in this book. In the famous battle between the prophet Elijah and the prophets of Baal, the center of that confrontation was the altar. In fact, this was not really a battle between a prophet of God and the prophets of Baal; it was a battle between the altar of Jehovah and the altar of Baal. You may know how that battle turned out. Let us just say that it was no contest: Jehovah powerfully and unequivocally demonstrated that He is the one and only true God. (See 1 Kings 18:17–40.)

AN ALTAR IS ANY PLACE WHERE WE INVITE, INVOKE, AND COMMUNE WITH SPIRITUAL POWERS.

One day, I was asked to pray over a young boy with cerebral palsy who was bound to a wheelchair. His mother wanted him to receive healing. As I and other believers were praying over him, the Lord revealed that a demonic spirit was involved in this infirmity. I asked the mother if she had ever been involved in the occult, and she put her head down and said, "Yes!" It turned out that she had been taking her young son to a psychic and witch. The moment we told the mother that she could no longer take her son to a psychic, the boy manifested the most evil spirit I had ever seen. He screamed, spat, and accused his mother of harming him. God told me that the spirit of palsy had a legal right to be there because it had been given permission through witchcraft, and the mother of this child was unwilling to repent and let go of this sin. I cannot tell you how many times I have witnessed a similar scenario with different people. In a sense, this mother had established an evil altar in her life, which gave permission to demonic spirits (including the spirit of infirmity) to operate in her life and attack her family.

Sometimes, we seem to have done all that we know to do to expel unclean spirits, and the demons still will not go. When dealing with demonic spirits that appear to be resilient and persistent, we must first establish whether or not the spirit has legal grounds to remain. There is a good example of this principle in the book of Acts:

> *Then certain of the vagabond Jews, exorcists, took upon them to call over them which had evil spirits the name of the Lord Jesus, saying, We adjure you by Jesus whom Paul preaches. And there were seven sons of one Sceva, a Jew, and chief of the priests, which did so. And the evil spirit answered and said, Jesus I know, and Paul I know; but who are you? And the man in whom the evil spirit was leaped on them, and overcame them, and prevailed against them, so that they fled out of that house naked and wounded.* (Acts 19:13–16)

You can see from this account that there were religious Jews who were attempting to exorcise a demonic spirit from a man, but they were approaching the demon incorrectly. They were using a ritualistic method and trying to adjure the spirit through *"the name of the Lord Jesus...whom Paul preaches."* The Greek word translated *"adjure"* in this passage is *horkizō*, which means "to force to take an oath" or "to administer an oath to."

These itinerant Jews were trying to make the spirit take an oath in order to get it to leave, and the Bible says that the spirit responded by saying, *"Jesus I know, and Paul I know; but who are you?"*

The seven sons of Sceva could not cast out the demonic spirit because they did not have the authority to do so, not being true believers in Jesus Christ. They tried to use the name of Jesus and the name of His apostle Paul, but they did not know Jesus themselves, and they were not in right standing with God. The evil spirit recognized all this; that spirit not only didn't come out, but it also turned on the men and severely beat them. Similarly, many people today are attempting to use a name that they do not really know. When they pray, they say, "In Jesus's name" merely as a ritual to get the things they desire; they are not truly submitted to the authority of that name. Praying in the name of Jesus is about more than simply the use of a phrase; it is about intimacy with Him and devotion to Him. We must make sure our lives are subject to the Lord Jesus before we can walk in His authority.

In this regard, one of the most important lessons I ever learned in deliverance ministry came one evening as I was conducting a Healing School. These schools are designed to teach believers about ministering healing and freedom to others as well as receiving healing for themselves. That particular evening was very interesting, to say the least. There was a woman in attendance who began to manifest demonically. She was disruptive, displaying continuous outbursts and expressions of mockery. After enduring this behavior for a while, I decided to confront the demonic spirit operating through her. (However, I cannot say I heard from God on this.) I was very frustrated, so I called her up to cast out the demon, and she began to laugh. This made me even more angry. Then a large number of people came up to the altar in a spiritual "gang rush" in an attempt to cast out the demon. The more the people yelled at the woman, the more she laughed, and the more chaotic the atmosphere became.

Unfortunately, we were operating in the flesh and not in the Spirit. Jesus said, *"That which is born of the flesh is flesh; and that which is born of the Spirit is spirit"* (John 3:6). On another occasion, Jesus said, *"How can Satan cast out Satan?"* (Mark 3:23). In the words of Dr. Martin Luther King Jr., "Darkness cannot drive out darkness; only light can do that."

After we had tried to deal with this demonic spirit for some time, I told everyone to back down and ignore her confrontation. Some people took her outside, and I continued ministering to the congregation. Eventually, they brought her back into the church. At that point, I spoke to the evil spirit, telling it that it was not allowed to speak anymore, and the woman became silent.

Afterward, I asked the Lord why the woman had not been instantly delivered. The first thing He said was that the evil spirit had legal rights to be there. The spirit operating in this woman was a spirit of chaos and confusion. And the more chaotic we became in dealing with her, the more legal grounds the spirit had to operate. Second, the Lord told me that by engaging in a spirit of frustration, we had been empowering the demonic stronghold. That day, I learned the importance of meekness. Jesus was never exasperated by demonic powers but always operated in the peace and strength of God. The Scriptures admonish us not to strive:

> *The servant of the Lord must not strive; but be gentle to all men, apt to teach, patient….* (1 Timothy 2:24)

When dealing with or confronting demonic spirits, we must always be led by the Spirit of God and operate in love. Bitterness, anger, fear, hatred, and chaos give ground to the accuser of the brethren and attract evil spirits. This is why some so-called deliverance ministers are ineffective in liberating people from bondage. They shout, scream, embarrass, and engage in drama that does nothing to help the person who is bound. In contrast, when our ministry has followed biblical principles according to the authority of the believer, we have seen countless people healed, delivered, and set free by the power of God.

WHEN DEALING WITH DEMONIC SPIRITS, WE MUST ALWAYS BE LED BY THE SPIRIT OF GOD AND OPERATE IN LOVE.

Some demonic spirits are sent to bring us frustration and exhaustion. I firmly believe that not every demon deserves our attention, time, and energy. One of Satan's greatest weapons is distraction. We must be careful not to become consumed by an attack that the enemy is launching against us but to remain focused on the Lord.

Let us seek to be fully aligned with the will of God for our lives. The Father desires for us to walk in freedom, and we must abide by His ways, and His ways alone, to experience complete freedom from any demonic stronghold. We need to be watchful not to attract familiar spirits, or to be ignorant partakers of Satan's intent to gain access into our lives by agreement and permission. We must repent of any ways in which we have deliberately or unconsciously invited "strange gods" into our lives. Let us humble ourselves before the Lord, and, without presumption, in the power of the Spirit, reject and expel any familiar spirits that would seek to operate through the law of attraction.

PRAYER OF RELEASE

Father God, I thank You for making a way for my freedom and eternal righteousness through Jesus's sacrifice and the power of His mighty and matchless name. I declare and decree that, according to John 8:36, Jesus Christ has already set me free. Therefore, I renounce any agreement with false gods that I have entered into under my own volition or out of ignorance. I declare that Satan has no power over me, for I am free in Christ. I thank You that I have full authority as a child of the most High God to cast out from me, my family, and my home anything that is not of You, and I do so right now. I decree that my mouth will speak the will of God for my life, according to His Word. I will speak only life, not death—which includes fear, discouragement, anxiety, chaos, and confusion. I invite the Holy Spirit to be my Guide and my Shield against the spirit of religion and all manner of deceptive practices and rituals. I exercise my spiritual authority, as given by Jesus in Luke 10:19, to overcome all the power of the enemy, in any form or fashion in which he comes. I declare that the enemy is subdued in all ways that concern me, my family, and my home. In Jesus's mighty name, amen!

INSIGHTS FOR OVERCOMING

1. The law of attraction works through counterfeit meditation, demonic magnetic attractions, the invoking of occult powers, spiritual "residue," the power of permission, and demonic altars.

2. The Holy Spirit will always lead us into all truth; the Spirit would never lead or tempt us to engage in behavior that is contrary to God's Word.

3. When we walk in the unconditional, agape love of God, demonic powers lose their hold and strength. God's love can break through all satanic attachments.

4. Bitterness, anger, fear, hatred, and chaos give ground to the accuser of the brethren, attracting evil spirits. When dealing with or confronting demonic spirits, we must always be led by the Spirit of God and operate in love.

PRACTICUM

1. Ask yourself the following questions proposed in this chapter: "What's pulling me?" "Who do I gravitate toward?" "What is a common characteristic of people in my circle?" Record your answers and reflect on whether you have any unhealthy attractions in regard to your hobbies, work, and relationships. If so, pray about these areas and write down how you will begin to remove these attractions from your life. Seek assistance from a trusted Christian counselor if you have been deceived into thinking you had permission to engage in adultery or other behavior that is contrary to God's Word.

2. Consider ways in which you may have given permission, authorization, or support to creating an atmosphere that is antithetical to the presence of God in your home. (If possible and appropriate, talk with your family members about this as well.) Areas to

consider include what you watch (on the Internet or TV), what you read, and the topics of your conversations. If you discover any areas that are negatively affecting the spiritual atmosphere of your home, determine how you will remove these negative influences in order to honor God with your whole life and protect your home from demonic attachments.

3. Have you been refusing to break an agreement with an ungodly "altar" (for example, holding on to occult associations or practices)? If so, repent immediately and ask God to completely cleanse you. Meet with godly, trusted spiritual leaders to pray about your desire to be totally free from these attractions and associations.

9

BREAKING UNGODLY SOUL TIES AND ATTACHMENTS

"Having therefore these promises, dearly beloved,
let us cleanse ourselves from all filthiness of the flesh and spirit,
perfecting holiness in the fear of God."
—2 Corinthians 7:1

In this chapter, we will take a deeper look at the implications and consequences of ungodly soul ties and other attachments. In this way, you can be alert to these associations in your own life and be prepared to renounce them and be set free from demonic oppression.

As I have prayed, interceded, fasted, and ministered to people who were struggling with familiar spirits, the Lord has given me increased revelation about soul ties. This is an area about which I receive many questions and prayer requests. Although my ministry is primarily concerned with the supernatural, the most prevalent questions I receive are in reference to relationships. This is an area that many people do not understand.

In chapter 5, we talked about how illegal soul ties are one of the portals that familiar spirits use to infiltrate our lives. If we are going to live in spiritual victory and freedom, we must break the power of ungodly soul ties. Remember that a soul tie is a bond involving the mind, will, and emotions of two individuals or a group of people. Such a bond can take place through intercourse, intimacy, and/or communion. We previously noted that there are good soul ties, as in the biblical example of Jonathan and David. Some additional positive examples from Scripture are Ruth and Naomi, Paul and Barnabas, and Paul and Timothy. There are other types of positive soul ties, such as the bond between a husband and wife in a godly marriage, or between a mother and a daughter, a father and a son, a spiritual mother and a spiritual daughter, or a spiritual father and a spiritual son. However, we know there are also negative soul ties where the bond or covenant is not authorized or sanctioned by God.

Severing ungodly soul ties is a necessity in anyone's life, but especially for a believer. Maintaining soul ties is dangerous to our lives and our growth in God. Christ Jesus shed His blood to give us victory over all demonic bondage, and we need to enter into the full freedom He has provided.

As we learned in a previous chapter, when an individual enters into a soul tie with someone, there can be a transference of demonic influence and oppression. Whatever spirits the individual's partner or friend was carrying now have the legal right to afflict them. This is why people who never dealt with a particular type of affliction or bondage will suddenly begin to struggle with that issue once a soul tie is established. Someone who never dealt with depression or anxiety will begin experiencing depression or anxiety. Or someone who never had a problem with pornography will begin dealing with lust and perversion. An illicit connection was made with something unlawful in the spiritual realm, and it opened the door to familiar spirits.

This transference is similar to the legal ramifications of a marriage where one spouse has bad credit and has racked up debts, but the other spouse is equally responsible under the law to pay back the money. Why? Because the marriage contract gives the first spouse's creditors access to their husband or wife.

Negative soul ties not only transfer sinful attitudes and tendencies from one person to another, but they also sometimes reshape people's whole personalities. A woman may be outgoing and jovial, but when the wrong man comes into her life, she suddenly becomes antisocial, closed in, or irritable. A man may be very responsible, dedicated, and disciplined, but when the wrong woman comes into his life, he becomes irresponsible, thoughtless, and reckless. Those bondages and strongholds have entered by way of an illegal soul tie.

> **CHRIST JESUS SHED HIS BLOOD TO GIVE US VICTORY OVER ALL DEMONIC BONDAGE, AND WE NEED TO ENTER INTO THE FULL FREEDOM HE HAS PROVIDED.**

CHANNELS OF UNGODLY SOUL TIES

ILLEGAL SEXUAL UNIONS

In 1 Corinthians 6:16, Paul wrote,

What? know you not that he which is joined to a harlot is one body? for two, says He, shall be one flesh.

The second part of this verse is a direct reference to Genesis 2:24, which says,

Therefore shall a man leave his father and his mother, and shall cling to his wife: and they shall be one flesh.

The Bible says that when a man or woman engages in sexual immorality with someone (in this particular instance, the Scripture is speaking of relations with a prostitute), he or she is actually joined to that person, and they become *"one flesh."* This is an ungodly soul tie that can produce devastating spiritual consequences. If you have sexual relations with someone you are not married to, you engage in an illegal union that is not sanctioned or blessed by God. Such a union opens the door to demonic soul ties and also to spiritual oppression. Many people are battling this distressing reality.

When people engage in sexual intercourse, they enter into a union that is recognized as a covenant in the spiritual realm. In biblical times, a couple would consummate a marriage through intercourse in order to legally seal a marriage. It was not the ceremony that made them a married couple but rather the sexual union. Because of the hypersexual culture we live in today, people do not often consider the gravity of sex before marriage or sex outside of marriage.

While having a sexual relationship outside of marriage creates harmful soul ties for both men and women, it seems that women, in particular, seem to suffer deep emotional consequences from them. The moment a woman sleeps with a man, she forms a spiritual bond with him. This is why, even if she goes on to another relationship or even gets married to another man, she still has a former "spiritual husband." Having a past spiritual husband or husbands can be a source of marital strife, sexual difficulties, and even illicit dreams that bring torment. In some marriages, it may literally feel like an entity is coming between the husband and wife, preventing them from becoming one as they were meant to be. I have counseled married people who cannot connect with their spouse because of a preexisting ungodly soul tie. This is because the former bond is blocking the new union.

In the insurance world, a preexisting medical condition may prevent someone from obtaining coverage. There are also preexisting conditions in the spirit. Again, a person can be affected by relationships that existed before their marriage. Their soul was connected to someone illegally, and this opened the door to familiar spirits that keep them trapped in the past.

In the apostle Paul's letter to the Corinthian church, he uses language that everyone at that time would have understood. Corinth was a city that was infamous for immorality. During the first century, temple prostitution was very common. In Corinth, there was a temple to Aphrodite that employed hundreds of temple prostitutes. "Priestesses" would be depicted in picture form to show men where the temple was. These priestesses would engage in sexually immoral acts to venerate the false deities that they worshipped. We know, according to Scripture, that they were actually worshipping demonic spirits.

But I say, that the things which the Gentiles sacrifice, they sacrifice to devils, and not to God: and I would not that you should have fellowship with devils.　　　　　　　　　　　　　　　　　　(1 Corinthians 10:20)

As the people engaged in this satanic worship, they would actually open their souls to demonic infestation and, in some cases, demonic possession. As far-fetched as this scenario might seem to us in modern times, many people are engaged in a similar practice today. Every time they forge an ungodly soul tie through sin, it brings with it a demonic power.

Paul wrote the above passage because the believers in the Corinthian church found themselves struggling with immorality. The city of Corinth was one of the most immoral cities in the first century, and this landscape of perversion had crept into the church. The church was even engaging in activities that not even the Gentiles participated in. That aspect alone indicates how demonic and disturbing this behavior was. It was a gross indictment on the Corinthian church, and Paul rebuked the Christians so they would repent and live according to their freedom in Christ. He knew the spiritual consequences of their behavior.

Years ago, when I was ministering overseas, a young woman came to me for prayer. She complained that although she was smart, attractive, and loved God, she could never get married. In fact, every time she entered a new relationship, something would happen that would sabotage it. She had been engaged several times, but each time, the wedding had been called off, even as late as a week before the scheduled ceremony. As this young woman looked at me with frustration, I told her that she needed to break ungodly soul ties. When I said that, she stared at me, and her eyes turned bloodshot. I prayed a simple prayer of deliverance over her to break the ungodly soul ties, and she was set free! The following year, she married a wonderful Christian man. We must stop the contagion of ungodly soul ties in our own lives and prevent them from affecting our children and subsequent generations.

WE MUST STOP THE CONTAGION OF UNGODLY SOUL TIES IN OUR OWN LIVES AND PREVENT THEM FROM AFFECTING OUR CHILDREN AND SUBSEQUENT GENERATIONS.

Let me include a note of caution: an ungodly soul tie is not the issue in all cases in which someone struggles with relationships or can't seem to get married. This is not a blanket statement that applies to everyone's situation. However, many times, problems in relationships like this are the consequence of an ungodly soul tie.

EYE-GATE AND EAR-GATE PORTALS

As we noted earlier, soul ties are not only formed through sexual unions. They can be formed through any type of spiritual, mental, emotional, or physical attachment. For example, soul ties can be created through the eye gates. When a person views pornography, the same spiritual principles apply. The word *pornography* comes from the Greek word *pornographos*, which literally means "writing about prostitutes"; it comes from *pornē*, "prostitute," and *graphein*, "to write."[20]

Jesus said, *"Whosoever looks on a woman to lust after her has committed adultery with her already in his heart"* (Matthew 5:28). Many believers have opened their lives to familiar spirits (including bonds with spiritual husbands or wives) through pornography. Make no mistake, to entertain pornography is to invite demonic spirits into your life. Such spirits can torment people for decades, even when their victims don't understand what is causing their oppression. Countless women and men have told me about being tormented in their sleep by evil spirits. Some people have reported a demonic entity visiting them in their dreams and their having a sexual encounter with this spirit. When these people wake up, they feel ashamed and defiled.

Not only eye gates but also ear gates can be the means of tying souls together. Even conversations can tether you to somebody. This was the case with Eve in the garden of Eden. Eve got into trouble because she entertained the false words of the serpent. She listened to a being who was full of evil, and because of what she entertained, she was seduced. (See Genesis 3:1–7.)

In chapter 5, I related the story of the man who became close friends with an individual who experienced constant calamity in his life. Through their friendship, that spirit of calamity transferred to the man's life, causing him to have a bad car accident. You may have close associations with people who are bringing a spirit of calamity or darkness into your own life. Many people are waiting for God to do something for them or to provide some relief to their circumstances, but God is saying, "No, you need to sever that soul tie; you need to break the connection that is giving the enemy access to your life." Once you break the connection in the name of Jesus, you will close the door to whatever has been tormenting you, and you will be able to move forward in God's purposes.

ASSOCIATIONS WITH MONITORING SPIRITS

Another way the enemy seeks to infiltrate our lives and thwart God's purposes is to use "monitoring spirits" to undermine us and draw us into demonic attachments.

First, we need to understand the difference between a "ministering spirit" and a "monitoring spirit." God sends us *ministering spirits,* or His angels, to assist us.

> *Are they* [angels] *not all ministering spirits, sent forth to minister for them who shall be heirs of salvation?* (Hebrews 1:14)

Angels are powerful spiritual beings, created by God, whom God sends to us as helpers. The Greek word translated *angelos* in Hebrews 1:14 means "a messenger." God will send human agents and angelic beings alike who have assignments to help you and encourage you. He will provide people who can give you exhortation, minister to you, and intercede for you. These people have been sent to cover you, not to expose you; they are there to strengthen you and to enable you to get where you are called to go. They are "ministering spirits."

But there are messengers of God, and there are messengers of Satan. God sends ministers, but Satan sends monitors. God sends intercessors, but the devil sends interceptors. Monitors and interceptors may be evil spirits or they may be human beings whom the enemy uses for his purposes. These monitors and interceptors seek to find out the areas where you are weak, where you are susceptible, where you can be accused of wrongdoing.

Many people have a misconception about Satan and how he operates. Contrary to popular belief, the enemy is not omniscient; he does not know everything. Remember, the devil is not God. He is a finite, created being, so the only way for him to obtain information about God's people is to do research and collect data. Therefore, he uses evil spirits to do surveillance on us in order to examine and gather information about us.

I will never forget an experience I had in my bedroom many years ago in which I was nearly suffocated to death. I could not breathe, and I was literally sinking down where I lay; I felt like darkness was hovering right above me. I screamed out, "I bind you, spirit of oppression!" When I declared those words, the feeling of suffocation literally broke off of me. At the same time, my spiritual eyes were opened, and I saw an entity that looked like an octopus or a jellyfish hovering over my bed. When that spirit saw me, it looked shocked because I was not "supposed" to be able to see him. I was not meant to know this demon was present. A successful spy never reveals their true identity and assignment.

I have just given an example regarding an evil spirit, but, as I wrote earlier, monitoring spirits often operate through people or use them for satanic purposes. You might ask, "Is there a scriptural basis for that idea?" Let's look at the biblical story of Nehemiah. Nehemiah was living as an exile in the Persian Empire with many other Israelites following the Babylonian invasions of Israel many years earlier during which the Babylonians had taken a number of the Jews captive. The Persians had subsequently defeated the Babylonians, and Nehemiah had been given the position of cupbearer to the Persian king, which was a highly trusted role. The Lord put it on Nehemiah's heart to go back to Israel and rebuild the broken walls of Jerusalem, which had been destroyed during the Babylonian assault. Nehemiah prayed and then asked the king if he could return to perform this task, and God's favor was upon him; the king granted Nehemiah's request and even provided building materials.

However, when some enemies of Israel heard of the rebuilding plan, they became very angry.

When Sanballat the Horonite, and Tobiah the servant, the Ammonite, heard of it, it grieved them exceedingly that there was come a man to seek the welfare of the children of Israel.　　　(Nehemiah 2:10)

Two of the individuals who sought to thwart Nehemiah's mission were Sanballat and Tobiah. Sanballat was a Horonite; he was likely from an area called Horonaim in Moab. In Hebrew, the name Sanballat means "strength." Sanballat had a companion named Tobiah, an Ammonite whose name signifies "Jehovah is good." These names seem ironic considering their opposition toward Nehemiah.

When Nehemiah began to rebuild the walls of Jerusalem, Sanballat and Tobiah immediately showed up. They were not there to offer support but to surveil those who were rebuilding the walls. They were there not to assist the Hebrew builders but to stop them. They wanted to hinder the work from going forth.

Throughout the challenges he faced while rebuilding the walls, Nehemiah recognized the character of his opponents. In Nehemiah 2, we see his discernment and strategic movements when his naysayers mocked the Jews' fervor in their work and accused Nehemiah of wrongdoing.

> *But when Sanballat the Horonite, and Tobiah the servant, the Ammonite, and Geshem the Arabian, heard it, they laughed us to scorn, and despised us, and said, What is this thing that you do? will you rebel against the king?* (Nehemiah 2:19)

To this, Nehemiah replied:

> *The God of heaven, He will prosper us; therefore we His servants will arise and build:* **but you have no portion, nor right, nor memorial, in Jerusalem.** (Nehemiah 2:20)

Nehemiah made it clear to Sanballat, Tobiah, and their cohort, Geshem, that they had no lot or part in the matter of rebuilding Jerusalem. They had no say in it, and they had nothing to do with this assignment and purpose, so he cut them off, denying Sanballat and the others access to him.

Likewise, we must take authority over monitoring spirits—whether demonic spirits or human beings—and cut off their access to us in the name of Jesus. Many believers confuse love with full access; yes, we are to love everyone with God's love, but this does not mean we are to give everyone close access to us. When Jesus's disciples asked Him why He spoke to the masses in parables, He said,

> *Because it is given to you to know the mysteries of the kingdom of heaven, but to them it is not given.* (Matthew 13:11)

WE MUST TAKE AUTHORITY OVER MONITORING SPIRITS— WHETHER DEMONIC SPIRITS OR HUMAN BEINGS— AND CUT OFF THEIR ACCESS TO US IN THE NAME OF JESUS.

Please note that being aware of the existence of monitoring spirits is not a reason to espouse fear or suspicion but rather to exercise wisdom and discernment. This will enable you to know the difference between a friend and a foe.

In this regard, we must understand that Satan is a false prophet; he is not capable of giving us real prophetic words from God. Thus, when the enemy says something to you through a monitoring spirit (either spiritual or human), he is not doing it to declare what *will be*. He is doing it to see what false idea *you might come into agreement with*. Again, Satan is not omniscient, so he has to observe you to know your desires and weaknesses. I like to use the example of "cookies" from computer science technology when explaining this type of spiritual warfare. In case you aren't familiar with this term, here is the technical definition:

> A small file or part of a file stored on a World Wide Web user's computer, created and subsequently read by a website server, and containing personal information (such as a user identification code, customized preferences, or a record of pages visited).[21]

For example, suppose you go to the website of a fast food restaurant and place an order. Then, when you log on to your social media page, suddenly,

---

21. *Merriam-Webster.com Dictionary*, s.v. "cookie," https://www.merriam-webster.com/dictionary/cookie.

advertisements for this restaurant keep popping up. Why? Because cookies were tracking your online activity. Cookie software investigates your interests and desires in order to determine what images and offers to present to you. The enemy uses a similar method: he presents temptations to us based on what we respond to and what we "bite," like a fish going after a certain bait.

Since the enemy is constantly trying to figure out what we are doing, we have to take authority over any satanic surveillance systems that may be monitoring us. We know that the devil is *the accuser of* [the] *brethren* (Revelation 12:10). The Greek word for *"accuser"* is *katēgoreō*, which means "to charge with some offense" like a plaintiff. The devil seduces us into sin, and then he records us sinning. He tempts us to do something and then tries to use what he told us to do against us. That is his modus operandi.

There may be people surrounding you who are operating under a spirit of surveillance. They are not there to support you or assist you. They are there to monitor you and gather information about you. They want to figure out what you are doing so they can hinder or completely block your assignment from God. Such people are influenced by monitoring spirits.

To do their monitoring, some people use the power of witchcraft, such as astral projection, where a person will project themselves through an astral plane to watch other people. The person using the astral projection will extend themselves remotely (in the spirit) into the rooms of people's homes to see what is going on.

I once encountered this type of monitoring spirit. Someone came to me while I was on one of my overseas ministry trips, and they thought they were being "prophetic," sharing with me the following: "I was in your house in the spirit." This person lived in one of the poorer areas of the world and had never traveled outside their country; they had never been to the United States even for one day in their natural life. Neither would they have had an opportunity to use Google maps or a similar method to view my home on the Internet. Yet, their description of the way my house looked and of my car and driveway was accurate. Right then, I had to take authority over that spirit. I said, "I take authority over you, you monitoring spirit. You are not a prophet. You are a demon. Who gives you the right to be in my house? I did not give you permission to be in my house. I did not give you permission to watch me."

Please understand that I am not saying that anybody who has a word of knowledge or a vision is a monitoring spirit. God gives spiritual gifts, and He can give a true prophet a word of knowledge or an insight or a vision concerning you in order to encourage and strengthen you. What I am saying is that sometimes what you are dealing with is not a ministering spirit but a monitoring spirit, and you need to know the difference for your spiritual well-being.

As a believer, you must walk in wisdom and learn to operate effectively in the gift of discernment from the Holy Spirit. (See, for example, 1 Corinthians 12:10.) Your level of discernment needs to be higher than it has ever been. You have to be able to recognize the presence of monitoring spirits operating through human beings. Be sure to read and study the Word and stay close to God in prayer, listening for His guidance and direction. Your senses must be exercised to discern between good and evil:

> *But strong meat belongs to them that are of full age, even those who by reason of use have their senses exercised to discern both good and evil.*
> (Hebrews 5:14)

Thus, you should be able to recognize, "This person is not someone I should let into my inner circle. I discern that is not their assignment." You don't need to submit a prayer request, divulge your dream or vision, or share your plans with everyone you meet but only those whom you trust in the Lord. Remember, some people are not sent to minister to you but to monitor you. Some people go to churches not with the intent to serve or to receive but to observe. I have seen this scenario play out many times. The first thing they want to discover is your weaknesses. In this sense, they have a "Delilah spirit."

Delilah, whom we read about in the book of Judges, had a monitoring spirit upon her. She was bribed by the Philistines to monitor Samson to find out the secret to his strength and how they might defeat him. (See Judges 16.) Those who harbor a monitoring spirit will inquire as to what areas you are struggling in and what you are dealing with. They will insist that they want to learn about your difficulties so they will know how to pray on your behalf. In reality, they are concerned about "preying," not "praying." They want to gather information on you so that information can be leveraged against you or be brought as an accusation against you.

Again, let me be clear: I am not saying that everyone who inquires about your well-being is a monitoring spirit because there are sincere Christian leaders and friends who want to support your spiritual growth and genuinely want to pray for you. Rather, I am referring to demonic spirits and people who are working under their influence. This is where our great need for discernment comes in.

AS A BELIEVER, YOU MUST WALK IN WISDOM AND LEARN TO OPERATE EFFECTIVELY IN THE GIFT OF DISCERNMENT FROM THE HOLY SPIRIT.

SPIRITS OF PREVENTION

Monitoring spirits may work in accordance with a spirit of prevention. When there is a calling on your life, the devil will do everything in his power to hinder you from reaching your destination. And one of the devices he employs is a spirit of prevention. No one ever taught me about this spirit in seminary or even in a Bible study; I discovered it in the trenches of full-time ministry. However, there are biblical examples of it, including one from the life of the prophet Daniel.

Daniel, living in exile in Babylon, was praying and fasting on behalf of the Jewish people when one of God's angels appeared to him. This angel told Daniel that his prayer had been heard when he first started praying, twenty-one days earlier. The heavenly messenger had been immediately sent from heaven with an answer, but he had been *"withstood"* by *"the prince of the kingdom of Persia."*

Then said he [the angel] to me, Fear not, Daniel: for from the first day that you did set your heart to understand, and to chasten yourself before your God, your words were heard, and I am come for your words. But the prince of the kingdom of Persia withstood me one and twenty days: but, lo, Michael, one of the chief princes, came to help me; and I remained there with the kings of Persia. Now I am come to make you understand what shall befall your people in the latter days: for yet the vision is for many days. (Daniel 10:12–14)

From Daniel's encounter with this angel, we learn that there is an unseen realm that affects human events and that the powers of darkness try to delay or prevent God's plans. Notice that the angel said, *"I am come for your words."* The ability to prompt angelic activity is another aspect of the spiritual authority we have as believers when we pray and make declarations according to God's will. However, for the purpose of this book, I want to focus on the fact that there was a spirit of prevention in the form of a demonic principality in the heavenly realm.

The Hebrew word translated *"withstood"* in the above passage is *'āmad*, among whose meanings are "to delay," "to stand still," "to stop (moving or doing)," or "to cease." There are spiritual forces that seek to create delay in our lives, to discourage us, and to convince us that God did not (and does not) answer our prayers. The devil is a liar! It is my firm belief that spirits of prevention and delay do not just operate in the heavenly realm, but they also operate through human agents. This is another reason why we must take inventory of our connections. One of the strategies of the enemy is to cause delay through insidious attachments.

SPIRITS OF SABOTAGE

Monitoring spirits not only seek to delay and prevent God's plans, but they also try to sabotage them. We noted earlier that *"evil communications [or companions] corrupt good manners ["character" NLT]"* (1 Corinthians 15:33). However, it is important for us to understand how that corruption functions in conjunction with soul ties. For example, the Bible says:

Make no friendship with an angry man; and with a furious man you shall not go: lest you learn his ways, and get a snare to your soul. (Proverbs 22:24–25)

The Scriptures tell us that we must not enter into a friendship with an angry man lest we adopt his ways and snare our souls. The Hebrew word translated *"friendship"* in this verse is *rāʿâ*, which, among many meanings, can signify "to associate with." This word has the connotation of sheep grazing together in a pasture. Many people don't realize that they are exposing themselves to a spirit of sabotage through wrong affiliations and connections. The word *sabotage* means "to deliberately destroy, damage, or obstruct (something), especially for political or military advantage."[22] Remember, familiar spirits seek to undermine our lives and destinies, hindering our callings and diminishing our spiritual vision and fervor.

The apostle Paul dealt with spirits of sabotage during his ministry. To give one illustration, Paul and Barnabas were preaching in the city of Iconium, and as they went about winning Jews and Greeks to the Lord, religious people stirred up strife:

> *But the unbelieving Jews stirred up the Gentiles, and made their minds evil affected* [bitter] *against the brethren.* (Acts 14:2)

Eventually, Paul and Barnabas had to flee to another region, where they continued to preach the gospel. (See Acts 14:7.) The sabotage could not prevent the gospel from being proclaimed wherever Paul went.

For another biblical example, let's return to the account of Nehemiah, who continued to face opposition from Sanballat, Tobiah, and others, even though he had refuted them.

> *But it came to pass, that when Sanballat, and Tobiah, and the Arabians, and the Ammonites, and the Ashdodites, heard that the walls of Jerusalem were made up, and that the breaches began to be stopped, then they were very angry, and conspired all of them together to come and to fight against Jerusalem, and to hinder it. Nevertheless we made our prayer to our God, and set a watch against them day and night, because of them.* (Nehemiah 4:7–9)

Nehemiah discerned that Sanballat and Tobiah were operating in a spirit of sabotage to keep the Israelites from fulfilling their assignment. Sometimes, people will persist in trying to monitor, delay, and sabotage our life or work. This is when we need to stand firm in the Lord, as Nehemiah did. In Nehemiah 6:1–3, we read:

---

22. Lexico.com, s.v. "sabotage," https://www.lexico.com/en/definition/sabotage.

Now it came to pass, when Sanballat, and Tobiah, and Geshem the Arabian, and the rest of our enemies, heard that I had built the wall, and that there was no breach left therein; (though at that time I had not set up the doors upon the gates;) that Sanballat and Geshem sent to me, saying, Come, let us meet together in some one of the villages in the plain of Ono. But they thought to do me mischief. And I sent messengers to them, saying, I am doing a great work, so that I cannot come down: why should the work cease, while I leave it, and come down to you?

Again, we see Nehemiah exercising discernment and not being tricked into an attachment with those who would do him harm and try to stop his God-given purpose. Years ago, when my wife and I were just beginning our ministry, we sought to connect with various pastors and ministries for support. At one point, we began to fellowship and partner with a few other ministries. There was one particular ministry that we were about to partner with on a deeper level when God gave my wife a dream in which this ministry gave us turtles. As soon as she awoke from the dream, she knew immediately what it meant and warned me that if we partnered with that group, it would bring years of stagnation to our own ministry. We never partnered with that ministry, and they eventually ceased operations. Had we been connected to them, it would have hindered our spiritual progress.

STOPPING THE CONTAGION

Most of us have experienced sickness in some form. Perhaps it was a common cold or a virus, such as the flu or the coronavirus. No matter what their degree of gravity, all viruses need a connection in order to transmit. Just as viruses can transmit between people who are in proximity to one another, demonic spirits can transfer through ungodly soul ties and attachments. One of the major ways we can stop the transmission of demonic assignments is by severing unauthorized connections.

God is saying that it is time for the church to be cleansed of unhealthy soul ties and associations. Until you sever a soul tie, it will be difficult to remove the connection that has given the enemy access to you. But there is good news: you can be free! You must make a decision that you will break these ungodly ties through the power of Christ. I invite you to do so right now.

PRAYER OF RELEASE

Father, in Romans 10:13, You said that whoever calls upon the name of the Lord will be delivered. You know all my needs. You know what binds, torments, and defiles me—every evil, unclean spirit. In the name of Jesus, I ask that You would deliver me and make me free of all ungodly soul ties and attachments. I declare that anything that was planted in my life by demonic powers is uprooted by the power of the blood of Jesus. Father, I speak annulment to every illicit union that was not established by You. I take authority over it, I renounce it, and I reject it. I break all soul ties with any and all spiritual husbands or wives and any nefarious spirit attached to them.

I also break the power of every monitoring spirit sent to my relationships and my home. I nullify every wicked spirit that has an assignment to infringe on my privacy or to impede the plans You have for me. I also deactivate any technology that is being used to surveil me against Your will, any ungodly surveillance system that has been sent to monitor me in order to report back to their "base" things that can be used to bring accusations against me.

Father, I thank You that I am released from every ungodly connection and association, including spirits of prevention and sabotage. As a child of God, I am released from every wicked tie. I am released from every spiritual bondage. I renounce everything that is causing perversion in my life, everything that is causing hindrances in my life, everything that is causing lack in my life. I receive the cleansing blood of Jesus for my spirit, soul, and body. I declare that I am totally free, in Jesus's name! Amen.

INSIGHTS FOR OVERCOMING

1. Maintaining soul ties is dangerous to our lives and our growth in God. Jesus Christ shed His blood to give us victory over all demonic bondage, and we need to enter into the full freedom He has provided.

2. Some channels of ungodly soul ties and attachments include illicit sexual relationships, eye-gate and ear-gate portals, and associations with monitoring spirits, including spirits of prevention and sabotage.

3. Satan is a finite, created being, so the only way for him to obtain information about God's people is to do research and collect data. He uses evil spirits to do surveillance on us in order to examine and gather information. To identify and remove monitoring spirits, we must walk in wisdom and learn to operate effectively in the gift of discernment from the Holy Spirit.

4. One of the major ways that we stop the transmission of demonic assignments is by severing unauthorized connections. You must make a decision that you will break ungodly soul ties and attachments through the power of Christ.

ASK YOURSELF

1. Which soul ties have you identified in your life that need to be broken? How will you give these areas over to God completely in order to sever those ties?

2. Have you encountered people in your life or ministry who were there to monitor rather than to minister? What happened in that situation? Based on what you have learned in this chapter, how will you respond to such circumstances in the future?

3. In accordance with Hebrews 5:14, how will you actively exercise your senses to discern good and evil?

10

RENOUNCING EVIL COVENANTS AND OATHS

*"What? know you not that your body is the temple of
the Holy Ghost which is in you, which you have of God,
and you are not your own?"*
—1 Corinthians 6:19

Previously, we explored the spiritual principle that the words we speak can invite and invoke spiritual powers—either benevolent or malevolent—to work in our lives. We also talked about the dynamics of generational curses and how these curses can have a devastating effect on people's lives both spiritually and physically. At this point, it is important for us to further understand the nature of covenants and oaths and their connection to the operation of familiar spirits. In this way, we will be able to renounce any evil covenants and oaths that are oppressing us.

POSITIVE COVENANTS AND OATHS IN THE BIBLE

We find the concept of covenants throughout the Scriptures, in both the Old and New Testaments. There are godly covenants and oaths as well as ungodly ones. In this chapter, we will mainly focus on the ungodly ones, but let us begin by looking at some positive examples. The first occurrence of the word *"covenant"* is in Genesis 6, where God made a covenant with Noah that he would be the progenitor of the human race after the flood:

But with you will I establish my covenant; and you shall come into the ark, you, and your sons, and your wife, and your sons' wives with you.

(Genesis 6:18)

The Hebrew word translated "*covenant*" in this verse its *berît*. Among its meanings are "covenant," "alliance," "pledge," and "agreement."

The first appearance of the word "*oath*" in the Bible is Genesis 26:28–29, where Abimelech of Gerar makes an agreement with Isaac:

We saw certainly that the LORD was with you: and we said, Let there be now an oath between us, even between us and you, and let us make a covenant with you; that you will do us no hurt, as we have not touched you, and as we have done to you nothing but good, and have sent you away in peace: you are now the blessed of the LORD.

The Hebrew word rendered "*oath*" is *'ālâ*, which literally means "an imprecation" or "a curse." It comes from a root word meaning "to swear "or "to adjure." An oath may be defined as "a solemn promise, often invoking a divine witness, regarding one's future action or behavior."[23] In the ancient world, oaths were often made before God, and there were specific curses or spiritual consequences associated with a refusal to honor or fulfill the oath.

When a covenant is established, it is typically accompanied by an oath. Usually, an oath is made to an equal or greater party to keep the one who made the oath accountable to the terms of the covenant. In the case of the covenant that God make with Abraham, the Lord could not swear by anyone greater, so He swore by Himself (see also Hebrews 6:13):

And the angel of the LORD called to Abraham out of heaven the second time, and said, By Myself have I sworn, says the LORD, for because you have done this thing, and have not withheld your son, your only son: that in blessing I will bless you, and in multiplying I will multiply your seed as the stars of the heaven, and as the sand which is upon the sea shore; and your seed shall possess the gate of his enemies; and in your seed shall all the nations of the earth be blessed; because you have obeyed My voice.

(Genesis 22:15–18)

---

23. Lexico.com, s.v. "oath," https://www.lexico.com/en/definition/oath.

Thus, we can think of covenants and oaths as solemn agreements that have spiritual implications and consequences. Throughout this book, we have talked about the law of agreement and how everything in the spiritual realm operates according to permission. Whatever we give permission to, we give power to. And such power is amplified with the incorporation of covenants and oaths.

COVENANTS AND OATHS ARE SOLEMN AGREEMENTS THAT HAVE SPIRITUAL IMPLICATIONS AND CONSEQUENCES.

UNGODLY OATHS AND COVENANTS

With this basic understanding of covenants and oaths, let us explore what kinds of covenants and oaths are ungodly, creating an opening for familiar spirits in people's lives.

SECRET SOCIETIES AND FRATERNAL ORDERS

Many people have unknowingly made oaths with demonic powers through their involvement with certain organizations. One of the most common examples of this is when people make oaths to secret societies (such as the Freemasons or Shriners). This is why the term "pledging" is often used in reference to joining such organizations. However, people are often unaware of the entity that they are coming into agreement with.

When I was a child, I was visiting at a relative's house and found a ritual book in the closet. I had no clue what the book was, but I was very inquisitive and brought it out to read. However, when I began to open this book, one of my relatives literally snatched it out of my hand and told me that I was not allowed to read it. This was very confusing to me at the time. I asked them why, but they never really answered me. Later, I discovered that this book was connected to Freemasonry. I also came to realize that the emblems on this particular ritual book were demonic and purportedly had connections to Baphomet and Pan, two demonic entities that were worshipped in the ancient world. Such connections to the occult have opened many people to familiar spirits and curses, such as calamity, mental illness, family strife, infirmity, and premature death, to name a few. I have ministered to countless people who were involved in such organizations, and I have heard many reports of calamity in the lives of their children and family members. Beloved, secret societies are rooted in idolatry, occultism, and spiritual darkness. God tells us that we are not to have any other gods before Him. (See Exodus 20:3.)

When I was in college, I considered pledging a fraternity. I knew that the fraternity did not align with my Christian beliefs, but there were many "Christians" who told me it was totally acceptable to join because, after all, "So-and-so is a Christian, and they pledged!" All the while, there was a lingering feeling deep within me that this was wrong. The night I was to pledge, I heard the voice of God speak to me, saying, "Son, you can pledge this fraternity, but you will have to do it without Me." The fear of God fell on me in a way that I cannot describe. I knew that if I proceeded to pledge, I would face severe spiritual consequences.

The apostle Paul admonished:

Be you not unequally yoked together with unbelievers: for what fellowship has righteousness with unrighteousness? and what communion has light with darkness? And what concord has Christ with Belial? or what part has he that believes with an infidel? And what agreement has the temple of God with idols? for you are the temple of the living God; as God has said, I will dwell in them, and walk in them; and I will be their God, and they shall be My people. Wherefore come out from among them, and be you separate, says the Lord, and touch not the unclean thing; and I will receive you, and will be a Father to you, and you shall be My sons and daughters, says the Lord Almighty.

(2 Corinthians 6:14–18)

We are commanded by God to refrain from agreements with ungodly things and people. Light is antithetical to darkness, and the two will never be in agreement. When born-again Christians connect to people, things, and organizations that are against God, they are communing with darkness. When Paul asked the rhetorical question, *"And what concord has Christ with Belial?"* the Greek word he used for *"concord"* was *symphōnēsis*, which means "agreement" or "accordance." This term is related to the English word *symphony*.

What are you in agreement with? What have you become synchronized with? What are you in harmony with? The Bible tells us not to touch what is unclean. This is not a reference to physical germs but to spiritual uncleanness.

UNGODLY BLOOD COVENANTS AND BONDS

Most of us have had a best friend or a "blood brother or sister" that we were deeply connected to at some point in our lives. Even if you did not have such a friend, you probably are familiar with the concept. These are people with whom we have entered into "soul ties." Remember, a soul tie is a strong bond with another person involving the mind, will, and emotions.

In the ancient world, people made covenants by mingling blood. It was common for two men to puncture their wrists and then join them together in order to bind themselves in a covenant relationship. In today's culture, covenants, including brotherhoods and sisterhoods, can be sealed in a much less dramatic way—they may simply be an agreement or bond with a friend, a close relative, a romantic partner, or even a mentor or mentee— but they are still significant.

Since such covenants can be positive or negative, we must be mindful of the vows that we make in the name of friendship. For example, I am very loyal to my friends. I am the type of person that you can befriend for life. However, this trait of fidelity, while having a positive side, has caused me many spiritual problems throughout the years. Why? Sometimes, I was loyal to things and people that were outside the will of God for me.

When I was a child, I had a very close friend, and I felt such a connection to him that I would follow him into situations and circumstances that were not good for me. I remember going to a party that I knew I should not go to simply because I wanted to support my friend. This was a disaster that opened me up to very negative spiritual consequences. Today, the two of us are no longer friends. Such experiences are why it is important to understand the nature of covenants and oaths, even ones we may not speak out loud but still establish in our hearts. How many times have we come into agreement with things without regard for their true nature or spiritual origin? Or how many times have we suffered spiritual, emotional, or even physical consequences because we were negligent in examining beforehand the spiritual implications of the agreements and relationships we made?

As long as an ungodly covenant or oath is active, the demonic realm has legal grounds to enforce the terms of that covenant or oath. Oaths keep us tethered to certain behaviors, circumstances, places, and even individuals until they are renounced and broken. This is why some people cannot leave the town or city they grew up in. This is why some people find it nearly impossible to break certain habits or patterns of behavior. This is why some people feel bound or obligated to certain individuals—no matter what. This can be the case with fraternal oaths; people feel compelled to do certain things for their fraternity brother or sorority sister even if it goes against their judgment or the Word of God in general.

As we discussed in the previous chapter, similar unhealthy covenants can occur in romantic relationships. I have seen situations in which a woman is not able to break away from her children's father, even after they are legally divorced or the relationship is severed prior to marriage. She finds herself unable to meet new men or develop healthy relationships, including platonic friendships. Even though the woman and her former husband are legally divorced, they have not broken the spiritual cord that binds them together. Satan uses this ungodly covenant to drive away new, productive relationships.

The same can be true of inordinate relationships between parents and children. Suppose a single mother tells her son that he must never allow any woman to come between them. "It's just you and me, little guy! Forever!" If the son, whether knowingly or unknowingly, accepts such a spiritual covenant, it may prevent him from ever getting married or else keep him from truly cleaving to his wife if he does get married. (See Genesis 2:24.) Behind such a situation are familiar spirits who act as spiritual enforcers or debt collectors, demanding that the terms of ungodly covenants and oaths be fulfilled.

UNGODLY OATHS KEEP US TETHERED TO CERTAIN BEHAVIORS, CIRCUMSTANCES, PLACES, AND EVEN PEOPLE UNTIL THEY ARE RENOUNCED AND BROKEN.

BITTER ROOT JUDGMENTS AND INNER VOWS

Years ago, I was introduced to the concept of bitter root judgments and inner vows by my pastor during a Bible study class. Honestly, at the time, I did not have a clue of what he was talking about, but I have since come to understand the concept very well. What do the terms "bitter root judgments" and "inner vows" refer to? And what do they have to do with oaths and covenants? When people go through traumatic experiences, especially when these traumas continue to affect them deeply, they have a tendency to make visceral judgments and/or make promises to themselves based on a negative motivation—that of never wanting to repeat the trauma of those painful circumstances. Therefore, they make statements like, "I will never get married again!" or "I will never be like my mom or dad!" These are classic examples of bitter root judgments and inner vows.

Yet the Bible teaches us:

Judge not, that you be not judged. For with what judgment you judge, you shall be judged: and with what measure you mete, it shall be measured to you again. And why behold you the mote [speck] that is in your brother's eye, but consider not the beam that is in your own eye? Or how will you say to your brother, Let me pull out the mote out of your eye; and, behold, a beam is in your own eye? You hypocrite, first cast out the beam out of your own eye; and then shall you see clearly to cast out the mote out of your brother's eye. (Matthew 7:1–5)

You have probably realized by now that the Bible is very accurate when it says, *"With what judgment you judge, you shall be judged."* If you do not believe this, ask any parent who judged their own father and mother as not being good parents or not raising their children in the most efficient manner. Many parents have had to repent for saying that they would never make the same mistakes their own parents made. Why? Because they often end up making similar mistakes. This can be due to the presence of bitter root judgments.

Jesus says that when we make an unrighteous judgment, we actually activate a spiritual law of reciprocity. We bind ourselves to becoming guilty of the same things for which we judged others. Why? In verse 5 of the previous passage, the Greek word for *"hypocrite"* is used to describe this phenomenon; *hypokritēs* refers to "a stage player," or "an actor under an assumed character." In the ancient world, a "hypocrite" was an actor who would use a mask to cover their face and augment their voice. But this mask inhibited the actor from seeing clearly. Bitter root judgments are actually a form of spiritual hypocrisy because we don't see our own failings and tendencies toward weakness. Thus, once we judge others, we bind ourselves to the very thing that we judged. When we make judgments based upon our hurt, disappointment, or pain, we unleash familiar spirits whose assignment is to ensure that we manifest the same behavior.

How do you recognize that you have a bitter root judgment? Such judgments, as the name suggests, spring from seeds of bitterness. For example, a young man who grows up without his biological father may feel rejected because of this void in his life. The wound of rejection that the young man incurs through his father's absence grows into a root of bitterness; from this bitter root, he makes a judgment against all fathers or all men who remind him of his father. The young man says, "I will never be like him!" Ultimately, this bitter root judgment opens the door to the same familiar spirits that caused his father to be absent in the first place. If the young man's father was an alcoholic or a workaholic, and he judged his father for this, the young man will often become the very thing he judged. (It is important to note that not everyone who has an absentee parent experiences feelings of rejection or bitterness that lead to being oppressed by familiar spirits.)

Whatever their origin, bitter root judgments and inner vows can invite demonic spirits into our lives. We must renounce these judgments and vows in order to break the demonic strongholds they create.

EVIL ALTARS

Another aspect of covenants and oaths are "evil altars." We briefly discussed evil altars earlier in this book, but I want to revisit this concept for the purpose of giving you a deeper understanding of how altars relate to covenants and oaths and how evil altars can be confronted and broken.

Ancient altars were essentially places of sacrifice. We noted how altars invite and invoke spiritual powers. When people make vows on an altar that is not from God, they come into agreement with familiar spirits. These agreements are like legal contracts in the spiritual realm. For a contract to be legally binding, there must be two elements: (1) All parties must agree about an offer made by one party and accepted by the other. (2) There must be an exchange of something of value.

In the case of vows made on an evil altar, the spiritual power being implored demands a sacrifice be made in exchange for a specific manifestation of that power. There are many technicalities to contracts, but, essentially, if a contract is not fulfilled, then the party who failed to meet their part of the obligation can be considered in breach of contract, unless the contract was broken on legal grounds.

There are instances where someone will make a sacrifice on an evil altar in order to obtain something that they desire, making an agreement with a demonic power. In exchange, they dedicate their immediate family and/or their descendants to that evil spirit. Thus, oaths and covenants can have generational implications. They can affect everyone attached to that bloodline for decades. This is why it is so important to recognize such oaths and covenants and renounce them accordingly.

WHEN PEOPLE MAKE VOWS ON AN ALTAR THAT IS NOT FROM GOD, THEY COME INTO AGREEMENT WITH FAMILIAR SPIRITS. THESE AGREEMENTS ARE LIKE LEGAL CONTRACTS IN THE SPIRITUAL REALM.

I remember an instance when I was praying for a woman who was dealing with chronic back pain. The Lord told me that this woman was dealing in the occult. When I asked her if she had any ties to the occult, she emphatically insisted that she did not know what I was talking about. Then, because of the word of knowledge God had given me, I asked her plainly, "Have you been involved with Hinduism?" and she said, "Yes!" She further said that she had been dedicated to the Hindu god Vishnu when she was a child and had received a ceremonial tattoo. Once I told her that this involvement was demonic and that the spirit that had been tormenting her had to loosen its hold, a male voice spoke out of her, saying, "I will never let her go!" The people around us were shocked when they heard that voice. I commanded the evil altar to be destroyed and the spirit to leave her, and she was totally set free!

Once we identified the evil altar that had given the familiar spirit of oppression legal rights, we knew how that spirit had gained access and could cast it out accordingly. How many people are being afflicted by an evil altar of which they are totally oblivious?

The cross of Jesus Christ is the legal ground upon which we can nullify every ungodly oath, agreement, covenant, or contract that was made on an evil altar and is affecting our lives in a negative way. We must declare that the finished work of Jesus cancels every ungodly agreement and releases us from the power of every evil altar, in the name of Jesus!

In order to do this, we must have a pure altar in our own lives. This means that we have a clear relationship with God, having good standing with our heavenly Father through Jesus Christ. There are several very important principles to understand regarding having a godly altar:

+ The power of a believer is based on the purity of their altar.

+ The purity of the altar determines the depth of your intimacy with God.

+ The purity of the altar determines the effectiveness of your spiritual authority.

We must realize that we are powerful agents in the earthly realm where Christ has given us dominion through His blood. Once we are born again, we automatically become citizens of the kingdom of God and can be used by the Lord in His purposes. Therefore, it should concern all of us as believers that any spiritual covenant we are involved in other than the new covenant in Jesus Christ, which He sealed by His shed blood, would frustrate or oppose God's plan for us. Anything that would cause us to be compromised in our spiritual walks will also limit our ability to hear and receive from God. What agreements we, as agents of the kingdom here on earth, come into will also have an effect on our representation of Christ.

Our bodies, minds, and souls are subject to God's use as vessels for His glory. The apostle Paul expressed it in this way:

> *What? know you not that your body is the temple of the Holy Ghost which is in you, which you have of God, and you are not your own?*
> (1 Corinthians 6:19)

Yes! Your body is the temple of the Holy Spirit, so you are accountable for how you use your body and what alliances you make with others through oaths, agreements, vows, or pacts. Christ does not want any part of us to be enslaved or in bondage to evil allegiances. We are called to glorify God in our bodies and in our spirits (see 1 Corinthians 6:20) because, as believers, all of us belong to the Lord.

THE CROSS OF JESUS CHRIST IS THE LEGAL GROUND UPON WHICH WE CAN NULLIFY EVERY UNGODLY OATH, AGREEMENT, COVENANT, OR CONTRACT THAT WAS MADE ON AN EVIL ALTAR AND IS AFFECTING OUR LIVES IN A NEGATIVE WAY.

IDENTIFYING COMPROMISE IN OUR LIVES

Any kind of spiritual uncleanness pollutes the soul. As we saw in the example of the woman who had been dedicated to the Hindu god, many people unknowingly come into bondage to oaths and covenants through traditions, rituals, yogic practices, psychic readings, demonic literature, idle conversations, and anything else they might encounter through their eye gates and ear gates that is not aligned with the will and Word of God.

These are all influences that can pollute your soul—the seat of your mind, will, and emotions. Remember, when you are born again, your spirit becomes right with God, but your soul and body must be disciplined with the help of the Holy Spirit. You must be intentional and deliberate about recognizing where you have permitted spiritual compromise to enter your life and renounce all ungodly covenants and oaths.

In the book of Acts, we read what happened when some residents of Ephesus believed in the Lord Jesus:

> *Many of them also which used curious arts brought their books together, and burned them before all men: and they counted the price of them, and found it fifty thousand pieces of silver.*   (Acts 19:19)

The spiritual realm is covenantal, and renouncing evil covenants, oaths, and altars is an essential part of being delivered from the power of familiar spirits. Remember, who or what you enter into a covenant with will determine who or what you give permission to occupy your spiritual (and sometimes physical) life. In the next chapter, we will further discuss the power of the blood of Jesus to liberate us from spiritual bondage of all sorts. However, it is critical that you also identify and reject any oath, ritual, right, vow, pact, or covenant that you have entered into or participated in that is not of God. Ask the Holy Spirit to reveal these covenants, oaths, and evil altars to you so that you can renounce them immediately. If you feel that there is an evil covenant, oath, or altar operating in your life, please pray this prayer right now.

PRAYER OF RELEASE

Father, in the mighty name of Jesus, I thank You for who You are and all that You have done in my life. I recognize that I have a new covenant with You through the sacrifice of Jesus Christ. Right now, I renounce and reject every evil covenant or oath that has operated in my life, whether with my knowledge or without it. I sever all agreements, pacts, brotherhoods, sisterhoods, or idolatrous practices that are antithetical to Your Word and ways and/or that deny that Jesus Christ is the Son of God and the only means to eternal salvation. Thank You, Lord, for filling every void in my life with the presence and power of the Holy Spirit. In the name of Jesus, amen!

INSIGHTS FOR OVERCOMING

1. Covenants and oaths are solemn agreements that have spiritual implications and consequences. Whatever we give permission to, we give power to. And such power is amplified with the incorporation of covenants and oaths.

2. People can create openings for familiar spirits through covenants and oaths from secret societies and fraternal orders, ungodly blood covenants and bonds, bitter root judgments and inner vows, and evil altars.

3. The power of a believer is based on the purity of their altar (a clear relationship of good standing with the heavenly Father through Jesus Christ); the purity of the altar determines the depth of your intimacy with God; the purity of the altar determines the effectiveness of your spiritual authority.

4. You must be intentional and deliberate about recognizing where you have permitted spiritual compromise to enter your life and renounce all ungodly covenants and oaths.

PRACTICUM

1. Ask God to reveal areas of your life where you have made ungodly covenants or oaths through your involvement in organizations or through personal bonds with others. As He reveals these areas to you, repent of them immediately and let go of your unhealthy ties to these relationships.

2. Identify any bitter judgments or inner vows you have made in the past, especially regarding your parents or other family members. Reject these judgments and vows and receive cleansing from them through the sacrifice and blood of Jesus Christ. Replace these bitter thoughts by quoting and memorizing Scriptures that reflect

God's good purposes for your life, such as Jeremiah 29:11: *"For I know the thoughts that I think toward you, says the* Lord, *thoughts of peace, and not of evil, to give you an expected end* [hopeful future]."

3. Commit today to establish a pure altar in your life:

    + Be intentional and deliberate about recognizing where you have permitted spiritual compromise to enter your life. Renounce all remaining ungodly covenants and oaths, ask for God's forgiveness, and accept His cleansing.

    + Surrender your whole self anew to God, recognizing that your body is the temple of the Holy Spirit and that *all of you* belongs to the Lord.

    + Make yourself accountable for how you use your body and carefully monitor any alliances you make with others through covenants, oaths, and other agreements.

11

THE POWER OF THE BLOOD

"For the life of the flesh is in the blood: and I have given it to you upon
the altar to make an atonement for your souls: for it is the blood that
makes an atonement for the soul."
—Leviticus 17:11

We cannot talk about removing the oppression of familiar spirits from our lives without discussing the power source that breaks the influence of these demonic entities. The ultimate spiritual "legal tender" that releases us from the obligation and penalty of sin and every curse associated with it is the blood of Jesus. That's right! The blood of Jesus paid our ransom, destroying the power of sin, poverty, sickness, and death!

THE SACRIFICE OF YOM KIPPUR (THE DAY OF ATONEMENT)

To help us understand the efficacy of the blood of Jesus, we will begin by looking at a vital spiritual principle found in the Word of God: *"the life of the flesh is in the blood"* (Leviticus 17:11). This principle was the basis of all the Old Testament sacrifices. Understanding sacrifice is a key to knowing how the spiritual realm operates and how to overcome familiar spirits.

Every year, the Israelites were required by the law of Moses to have a sacrifice made on their behalf to atone for and cover their sins.

Also on the tenth day of this seventh month there shall be a day of
atonement: it shall be a holy convocation to you; and you shall afflict

your souls, and offer an offering made by fire to the LORD.

(Leviticus 23:27)

Once a year, the high priest would take two animals, the scapegoat and the sacrificial goat. He would transfer the sins of Israel onto the scapegoat by the laying on of hands and banish it into the wilderness. The other goat would be used as the sacrifice for the sin offering; its blood would be poured upon the mercy seat in the holy of holies. (See Leviticus 16:5–22.)

This sacrifice was the spiritual atonement for Israel's sin for that year, but the sacrifice had to be observed every year in order for the Israelites to remain in forgiveness and right relationship with God. The yearly sacrifice was insufficient to cleanse the people permanently because they would continue to sin every year, and thus a perpetual sacrifice was required.

JESUS, OUR SACRIFICIAL LAMB

However, God had a plan of redemption that would solve the problem of sin once and for all: His only begotten Son, Jesus, would make the sacrifice for the sins of the world. This sacrifice would not need to be repeated but would fulfill all righteousness:

For the law having a shadow of good things to come, and not the very image of the things, can never with those sacrifices which they offered year by year continually make the comers thereunto perfect. For then would they not have ceased to be offered? because that the worshippers once purged should have had no more conscience of sins. But in those sacrifices there is a remembrance again made of sins every year. For it is not possible that the blood of bulls and of goats should take away sins. Wherefore when He comes into the world, He says, Sacrifice and offering You would not, but a body have You prepared Me: in burnt offerings and sacrifices for sin You have had no pleasure. Then said I, Lo, I come (in the volume of the book it is written of Me,) to do Your will, O God. Above when He said, Sacrifice and offering and burnt offerings and offering for sin You would not, neither had pleasure therein; which are offered by the law; then said He, Lo, I come to do Your will, O God. He takes away the first, that He may establish the second. By the which will we are sanctified through the offering of the body of Jesus Christ once for all. (Hebrews 10:1–10)

The Bible calls Jesus *"the Lamb slain from the foundation of the world"* (Revelation 13:8). This is a reference to the Passover lambs that were slain at the time of the exodus from Egypt. Following God's instructions, the Israelites applied the blood of these lambs to the doorframes of their homes so they would be delivered from the death angel. (See Exodus 12:1–28.)

Jesus's blood was the only blood worthy to pay the price for our sin because His blood is sinless. Jesus was the substitutionary and propitiatory sacrifice that removed the penalty of sin, broke the curse of the law, and turned the wrath of God away from us. It is as if, the moment we were born again, we received a spiritual blood transfusion. Jesus's sinless, spotless, pure blood removed every stain and blemish from our spiritual lives—we were cleansed completely! Hallelujah!

The accuser of the brethren understands this spiritual law very well. That is why he hates the blood of Jesus. Christ's blood discharges every debt that humankind could ever incur. When we place our faith and trust in Jesus as our Sacrifice, and when we confess and repent of our sins, His blood cleanses us from all unrighteousness:

If we confess our sins, He is faithful and just to forgive us our sins, and to cleanse us from all unrighteousness. (1 John 1:9)

The blood of Jesus is more powerful than anything we could ever fathom or imagine. His blood is necessary for breaking demonic strongholds off of your life and the lives of your family members. Why? Because the very life of Christ was and is in the blood! Christ is greater than all the powers of darkness combined. His name and His blood are stronger than any bondage or affliction that we could ever experience.

THE BLOOD OF JESUS IS MORE POWERFUL THAN ANYTHING WE COULD EVER FATHOM OR IMAGINE.

THE POWER OF PLEADING THE BLOOD

Just as a defendant pleads their case in a human court of law, you and I can plead the blood of Jesus in the courts of heaven. When we do this, something supernatural happens. The hosts of hell are reminded of the defeat they endured and the victory we have in Christ.

The question remains, why are so many Christians still experiencing the implications of a curse in their lives? That is a very good question. Christ has redeemed us from the curse, but as participants in the new covenant, we must appropriate the promises associated with that covenant. This is a spiritual reality we must apply to every area of our lives. We must declare that the blood of Jesus has cleansed us from all unrighteousness, and therefore we stand before God holy and unreprovable. We no longer have to surrender to the lies of the enemy. We no longer have to live in bondage or defeat.

> *Christ has redeemed us from the curse of the law, being made a curse for us: for it is written, Cursed is every one that hangs on a tree: that the blessing of Abraham might come on the Gentiles through Jesus Christ; that we might receive the promise of the Spirit through faith.*
> (Galatians 3:13–14)

Jesus ratified the new covenant, with all its promises and benefits, with His own blood. After we are born again, we must make a claim on Christ's finished work by invoking His blood. "Pleading the blood of Jesus" is more than just a cliché. It is a spiritual revelation. Every time we point to the sacrifice of Jesus on our behalf and on behalf of our family members, we are pleading His blood over our lives and the lives of those we love. If you are experiencing oppression in any area of your life, apply the blood!

THE LIFE IS IN THE BLOOD

> *For the life of the flesh is in the blood: and I have given it to you upon the altar to make an atonement for your souls: for it is the blood that makes an atonement for the soul.*
> (Leviticus 17:11)

Previously, we saw that *"the life of the flesh is in the blood."* We established that this spiritual principle is the basis of all sacrifice in the Bible. We further noted that the shed blood of Jesus Christ was the sacrifice of atonement that was acceptable to God to take away the curse of sin and death from our lives completely and permanently.

It is important to understand the deep spiritual ramifications of the blood of Jesus. Consider the nature of human blood. Not only does blood deliver oxygen and nutrients to all the vital organs in the body, but it also carries deoxyribonucleic acid, or DNA. What is the significance of DNA? First, let us define what DNA actually is:

> A self-replicating material that is present in nearly all living organisms as the main constituent of chromosomes. It is the carrier of genetic information. Each molecule of DNA consists of two strands coiled around each other to form a double helix, a structure like a spiral ladder.[24]

DNA is the code of all biological life. This is why blood is so important from a natural perspective. The question is, what is the much deeper significance of the blood of Jesus? Through Christ's blood, we have received the spiritual DNA of the heavenly Father within the fiber of our spiritual being. The very life of God flows in and through us by virtue of the blood of Jesus and the power and presence of the Holy Spirit.

Demons are focused on blood because they know that the life is in the blood. Have you ever noticed that in all the horror and vampire movies, the emphasis is on blood? In these films, the vampire consumes blood. The occultist or warlock searches for a virgin or innocent person to sacrifice in order to invoke evil spirits. Within witchcraft and occultism, there is a requirement for blood sacrifice as a source of spiritual power. Often, when people are being promoted in the occult world, they will begin to engage in blood sacrifices to solidify and increase their power. The sacrifice will usually become more and more aberrant and disturbing as their thirst for power and success increases. They may even sacrifice a family member or a young child.

---

24. Lexico.com, s.v. "DNA," https://www.lexico.com/en/definition/dna.

This is also why the sin of abortion is so egregious in the sight of God. It is essentially the blood sacrifice of unborn babies on the "altar of Molech." Molech, or Moloch, was "a heathen god worshiped especially by the Ammonites with gruesome orgies in which little ones were sacrificed."[25] God actually judges nations based upon the shedding of innocent blood. But the pure blood of Christ Jesus was shed for our sins once and for all, and it has established for all who believe in Him an eternal covenant relationship with God. With repentance and faith, we can receive forgiveness and a new life in Christ.

> **THE VERY LIFE OF GOD FLOWS IN AND THROUGH US BY VIRTUE OF THE BLOOD OF JESUS AND THE POWER AND PRESENCE OF THE HOLY SPIRIT.**

THE BODY AND BLOOD OF JESUS IN COMMUNION

Then Jesus said to them, Verily, verily, I say to you, Except you eat the flesh of the Son of Man, and drink His blood, you have no life in you. Whoso eats My flesh, and drinks My blood, has eternal life; and I will raise him up at the last day. For My flesh is meat indeed, and My blood is drink indeed. He that eats My flesh, and drinks My blood, dwells in Me, and I in him. (John 6:53–56)

One of the most controversial statements our Lord made is found in John 6:53: "*Verily, verily, I say to you, Except you eat the flesh of the Son of Man, and drink His blood, you have no life in you.*" Was Jesus advocating cannibalism? Of course not! Instead, there is a deep spiritual meaning to this statement. It essentially refers to what we would call Communion (the fulfillment of the Passover Seder). As we "partake" of Jesus's body and blood by accepting His sacrifice on the cross and by embracing the spiritual "elements" of that sacrifice, we are in effect eating and drinking His body and blood. From a spiritual standpoint, when we take Holy Communion,

---

25. Tenney, *Zondervan Pictorial Bible Dictionary*, 550.

we are consuming the supernatural life of Jesus and being filled with His fullness. I recognize that people have different doctrinal understandings of what this exactly means. However, suffice it to say that we must have a revelation of who Jesus is and what He accomplished on the cross through His body and blood.

In 1 Corinthians 11:17–31, Paul gives us great insight into Communion, or the Lord's Supper. Let us look at a portion of that passage:

> *And when He [Jesus] had given thanks, He broke it [the bread], and said, Take, eat: this is My body, which is broken for you: this do in remembrance of Me. After the same manner also He took the cup, when He had supped, saying, This cup is the new testament [covenant] in My blood: this do you, as often as you drink it, in remembrance of Me.* (1 Corinthians 11:24–25)

Jesus's body was broken so that our bodies could be healed. His blood was shed so that our lives could be cleansed. Holy Communion is not simply a ceremony or a ritual; it is indeed a prophetic act that releases supernatural deliverance and healing to those who partake in it. In fact, I believe that Communion is a weapon of mass destruction to the kingdom of darkness. When we rightly discern the body of Christ and receive the elements with a spirit of reverence and revelation, it literally releases heaven on earth.

HEALING ISSUES OF BLOOD

Years ago, my wife, Gloria, was diagnosed with gestational diabetes during one of her pregnancies. The first thing we did when we received this diagnosis was to take Communion. We applied the blood of Jesus to her body and declared, "The blood of Jesus is diabetes-free; therefore, Gloria's blood is diabetes-free, also, in the name of Jesus." Then we ate the Communion elements together. The following day, Gloria went to the doctor, and she was free of diabetes! This healing came about without her making any dietary changes. Hallelujah! The life of Jesus is in the blood!

Years ago, when I first began pastoring, we held a large meeting, and the Lord gave me a word of knowledge about women who had issues of blood. I called all women with such conditions to the altar for prayer. I was surprised when the altar became filled with women of different ages and ethnic backgrounds who were having problems in this area. I began to renounce and cast out the spirit of infirmity and declare the blood of Jesus over those specific issues of blood. Many people reported an instant manifestation of healing in their bodies.

At a conference we held some time ago, a woman was in attendance who had recently been diagnosed with fibroids. This condition was causing a myriad of health problems and frustrations for her. As she sat in the session where I was teaching about the blood of Jesus, she felt the fibroids begin to melt, so she ran to the bathroom and began passing the fibroids out of her body. The blood of Jesus is more powerful than any sickness plaguing your life today.

As we have seen, there is supernatural power in the blood of Jesus Christ. The blood is the devil's worst nightmare. When we properly apply Jesus's blood to our lives, it can revoke the legal claims of familiar spirits and cover our homes and bloodlines with a hedge of supernatural protection.

> But God commends His love toward us, in that, while we were yet sinners, Christ died for us. Much more then, being now justified by His blood, we shall be saved from wrath through Him. For if, when we were enemies, we were reconciled to God by the death of his Son, much more, being reconciled, we shall be saved by his life.　　(Romans 5:8–10)

As you pray the prayer of release for this chapter, apply the blood of Jesus as full payment for every outstanding spiritual debt and demonic lien that has come against your destiny and future.

PRAYER OF RELEASE

Father, I plead the blood of Jesus over my mind, my will, my emotions, and my body. I break the power of the enemy in my life. I apply the blood of Jesus as the legal tender and full payment against every outstanding spiritual debt I owe. In Jesus's name, all demonic liens against me are released, including sickness liens, barrenness and miscarriage liens, mental illness liens, poverty liens, and any other type of demonic lien. Father, right now, I release all bitterness and unforgiveness in my heart. I forgive every person whom I have held in the captivity of unforgiveness, including myself, in accordance with Matthew 6:12, which says, *"Forgive us our debts, as we forgive our debtors."*

Father, I thank You in advance that the things I have been praying about and believing You for are now becoming a reality in my life. I receive, as a result of the cleansing power of Jesus's shed blood on the cross, the full manifestation of my identity in Christ so that I can begin to fulfill my purpose and assignment from this day forward. I release all shame, guilt, and condemnation, for they are no longer my portion. I thank You, Jesus, for going to the cross to destroy the works of the devil in my life. I thank You, Lord, that the enemy is already defeated. I claim my full freedom, in Jesus's mighty name! Amen.

INSIGHTS FOR OVERCOMING

1. A vital spiritual principle found in the Word of God is *"the life of the flesh is in the blood"* (Leviticus 17:11).

2. Christ's blood was the only blood worthy to pay the price for our sin because His blood is sinless. He was the substitutionary and propitiatory sacrifice that removed the penalty of sin, broke the curse of the law, and turned the wrath of God away from us.

3. Holy Communion is not simply a ceremony or a ritual; it is a prophetic act that releases supernatural deliverance and healing to those who partake in it. Communion is a weapon of mass destruction to the kingdom of darkness.

4. There is supernatural power and healing in the blood of Jesus Christ. When we properly apply Jesus's blood to our lives, it can revoke the legal claims of familiar spirits and cover our homes and bloodlines with a hedge of supernatural protection.

ASK YOURSELF

1. After reading this chapter, has your perspective on appropriating and applying the blood of Jesus to your life changed? If so, in what way(s)?

2. How do you respond to this statement: "Holy Communion is not simply a ceremony or a ritual; it is indeed a prophetic act that releases supernatural deliverance and healing to those who partake in it"?

3. Are you applying the blood of Jesus to every area of your life? How will you apply His blood to a need in your life today?

12

THE MIND:
OUR SPIRITUAL BATTLEGROUND

"(For the weapons of our warfare are not carnal,
but mighty through God to the pulling down of strong holds;)
casting down imaginations, and every high thing that exalts
itself against the knowledge of God, and bringing into captivity every
thought to the obedience of Christ."
—2 Corinthians 10:4–5

Contrary to what many people believe, spiritual warfare is not some mystical or ethereal activity that takes place in a distant dimension. Rather, the battlefield of spiritual warfare is in *the mind*. Most of what the enemy attempts to do to bring God's people into bondage involves our thoughts. As we seek to become free of familiar spirits and keep them from gaining a foothold in our lives, we must be sure we understand where the spiritual battles are fought and won.

In 2 Corinthians 10:5, Paul uses a very interesting Greek word for the concept translated as *"imaginations."* The word is *logismos*, one of whose definitions is "a reasoning: such as is hostile to the Christian faith." Thoughts influenced or planted by the enemy are often camouflaged as a logical way of thinking, but in actuality they are insidious and malevolent. Familiar spirits try to sow demonic images, ideas, and perceptions into our minds. They use destructive thought patterns to enslave their victims to attitudes and mindsets that produce despair, defeat, and, in some cases, death.

The root word of *logismos* is *logos*. With regard to speech, this term can refer to "a word, uttered by a living voice; [it] embodies a conception or idea." Accordingly, the thoughts that the enemy implants in the minds of believers become like "voices in our heads." Have you ever felt like a voice other than God's was speaking to you? I am not talking about text-book schizophrenia where a person actually hears voices. I am referring to thoughts and impressions that operate in our minds. Unless we are aware of the origin of erroneous thoughts and learn to resist them, they can become a powerful voice that has the ability to negatively influence our lives.

FALSE PARADIGMS

I cannot emphasize enough the importance of understanding the dynamics of spiritual warfare with regard to the mind. Demons seek to express their evil assignments through the thoughts and lives of people who are willing to host them, whether knowingly or unknowingly. The goal of the enemy is to spiritually distract or even assassinate people to prevent them from fulfilling their God-given assignments and destinies.

Familiar spirits actually operate within the framework of our thought patterns and paradigms. A "paradigm" is simply a pattern of thinking. For example, a person can have a victim-based paradigm that suggests they are entitled to help and assistance all the time and at all costs. People who possess such a paradigm often battle with ingratitude and entitlement. They imagine that the world owes them a tremendous debt. They may even feel hurt or rejected if you do not give them what they desire. Why? Because their paradigm is deeply entrenched in the fabric of their thoughts, behaviors, and even personality.

When a familiar spirit infests a person's paradigm, it becomes extremely difficult for that person to distinguish between their own thoughts and the thoughts planted by the enemy. This is why the discerning of spirits is such an important gift of the Holy Spirit with regard to healing and deliverance. Sometimes people are oblivious to the fact that much of their mental framework has been infected by demonic spirits. Often, when I have a deliverance or healing session with someone, I ask them questions about their life and experiences, and I follow up with probing questions about their current mindset. In most instances, the people I counsel have been totally unaware of the impact demons have had on the way they think.

We noted previously that we must train ourselves to know the difference between the voice of God and the voice of the enemy. That is why Jesus said, *"My sheep hear My voice, and I know them, and they follow Me"* (John 10:27). Earlier, while describing the relationship between sheep and their shepherd, Jesus said, *"A stranger will they not follow, but will flee from him"* (verse 5).

The enemy of our souls often attempts to impersonate or muffle God's voice in the lives of believers. This is where the demonic realm literally thrives. The goal of familiar spirits is not just to attack us physically or even spiritually but to cause us to embrace a mindset that is contrary to the Word of God. Once someone embraces a false mindset, it becomes a spiritual stronghold or fortress that can be inhabited by demonic powers. The voice that we heed becomes the voice that dominates us.

EVEN THOUGH WE ARE IN A TOUGH SPIRITUAL BATTLE INVOLVING OUR MINDS AND THOUGHTS, WE HAVE SPIRITUAL WEAPONS THAT ARE GREATER THAN THOSE OF OUR ENEMY.

As we have seen, the enemy's purpose for establishing strongholds in our lives is to gain access and influence. Again, whatever has access to our lives has the ability to influence us; and whatever has influence over us controls our destinies. The devil cannot diminish your God-given destiny, but he can seek to divert and/or discourage you from reaching it. However, even though we are in a tough spiritual battle involving our minds and thoughts, we have spiritual weapons that are greater than those of our enemy.

WHOSE VOICE ARE YOU LISTENING TO?

Countless times, I have conversed with Christians who have told me, "God said…" when He actually never said it. How do I know that? Because what God supposedly said did not align with His Word or His ways. Some people honestly believe that God is speaking to them, but they are being led and influenced by familiar spirits that are simulating His voice in order to lead these people into confusion. Such instability is a demonic stronghold in a person's mind that alienates them from a life of freedom and victory. It is as if the person is being attacked from within themselves.

For example, a person may say that God told them to join a church or accept a position on a job, only to come back a few days later and announce, "God has released me!" Wait! What? Did God change His mind that fast? Did He change His mind at all? Demonic thoughts are like shifting shadows. (Contrast James 1:17.) This is why so many believers deal with inconsistency in their thoughts and emotions. This is the cause of so much inner turmoil and confusion in the lives of millions of people all over the world. To be under the influence of familiar spirits is to be like a wave *"tossed to and fro"*:

> *That we hereafter be no more children, tossed to and fro, and carried about with every wind of doctrine, by the sleight of men, and cunning craftiness, whereby they lie in wait to deceive; but speaking the truth in love, may grow up into Him in all things, which is the head, even Christ.* (Ephesians 4:14–15)

Beloved, not every voice in your head is the voice of God. In fact, God does not often speak to us in our heads at all; He mainly speaks to our spirits. Please do not misunderstand me: at times, we all make mistakes and miss what God is telling us. But if someone is constantly saying, "God said," and then, a short time later, insisting that God is saying something completely different, that person is probably dealing with a familiar spirit.

God's voice does not create mental, spiritual, or emotional instability in people. His voice is steadfast, producing peace, not confusion! The Bible says, *"For God is not the author of confusion, but of peace, as in all churches of the saints"* (1 Corinthians 14:33). If we think we are hearing God's voice, yet this voice is producing confusion in our lives instead of peace, we can rest assured that it is not the voice of God.

IDENTIFY THE SOURCE

When I was growing up, I was quite a rambunctious child, to say the least. I couldn't sit still for five minutes. I would often be outside playing with sticks or climbing trees. My siblings always laughed about my adventures and antics. In fact, they still laugh about them today!

Sometimes I would shadowbox in the house or outdoors. When you shadowbox, you swing at an imaginary person, so you're essentially punching the air. Sometimes boxers use this method to train, but I would do it to release pent-up energy. What I want to emphasize is that a shadowboxer's opponent is invisible. Yet, even though they are swinging at an opponent who only exists in their minds, they are still expending time and exerting energy.

In a similar way, countless people are exhausted from a spiritual fight that they cannot seem to win because they have yet to identify where the battle comes from. Many believers do not realize that what they are fighting against is actually in their own minds or imaginations. They are essentially engaged in spiritual shadowboxing.

If we allow him to, the enemy uses our experiences, traumas, and circumstances to plant thoughts and suggestions in our minds, thereby constructing demonic strongholds. Each additional thought becomes a brick in the fortress that Satan attempts to build to house his hordes of hell, haunting and tormenting people from within. These are spiritual attacks by familiar spirits whose goal is to bring about perpetual condemnation, alienation, and isolation.

This is one of the reasons why many Christians deal with depression. The enemy attacks their minds and emotions, which give way to a spirit of despair and even death. This statement is by no means a trivialization of depression; many people have suffered the devastation of mania and depression, but I believe that there are spiritual root causes to such conditions, and I also believe there is a way out.

During my first year in ministry, a feeling of despair came over me. This feeling was inexplicable because God was doing great things in my life; there should not have been a reason to despair. I did not realize that this was a demonic attack. One of the ways you know that you are under a demonic attack is that there is incongruence between your circumstances and how you actually feel. If you suddenly feel like giving up on life or that no one loves you, this is an indication that you are being afflicted by familiar spirits.

In my case, I literally despaired of life. I wondered if God had even called me. It was only through revelation from the Lord that I recognized I was dealing with a spirit of despair, as well as a Jezebel spirit. God opened my eyes to what I, as well as many other church leaders, had unknowingly experienced. To better understand how this happens, let's look at an example from the life of the prophet Elijah, who was afflicted by the same spirit:

> *And Ahab told Jezebel all that Elijah had done, and withal how he had slain all the prophets with the sword. Then Jezebel sent a messenger to Elijah, saying, So let the gods do to me, and more also, if I make not your life as the life of one of them by tomorrow about this time. And when he saw that, he arose, and went for his life, and came to Beersheba, which belongs to Judah, and left his servant there. But he himself went a day's journey into the wilderness, and came and sat down under a juniper tree: and he requested for himself that he might die; and said, It is enough; now, O* Lord, *take away my life; for I am not better than my fathers.* (1 Kings 19:1–4)

Elijah had been attacked by a spirit of oppression and depression. The Bible says that he *"requested for himself that he might die."* You know it is pretty bad when you ask God to take your life! This attack was in the form of a word curse (a form of witchcraft) spoken from the mouth of Queen Jezebel. Can you imagine a powerful prophet who had just experienced a major victory running from Jezebel and having suicidal thoughts and prayers? As irrational as this episode in Elijah's life may seem, such a reaction is a very common occurrence in the lives of millions of people. Witchcraft attacks the mind, producing feelings of despair, hopelessness, rejection, and suicide. We must learn to recognize that such thoughts are indeed demonic.

The beautiful aspect is that once you have identified the source of the attack, you can take authority over the demonic spirits. When you have a revelation of who you are in Christ and your authority as a believer, you can sever ties with familiar spirits that have been assigned to you and have been attacking you unceasingly. Friends, we must tear down these demonic strongholds!

> ONCE YOU HAVE IDENTIFIED THE SOURCE OF THE ATTACK,
> YOU CAN TAKE AUTHORITY OVER THE DEMONIC SPIRITS.

BREAKING MENTAL AND EMOTIONAL STRONGHOLDS

To break mental and emotional strongholds, we must not only understand where the battles are fought, but we must also make sure we recognize the realm of the devil's playground. Let's return to Ephesians 6:12, which we examined in chapter 1 of this book:

> *For we wrestle not against flesh and blood, but against principalities, against powers, against the rulers of the darkness of this world, against spiritual wickedness in high places.* (Ephesians 6:12)

I mentioned previously that the Greek word translated "*darkness*" is *skotos*. One of the literal meanings of *skotos* is "darkened eyesight or blindness," and one of its figurative meanings is "ignorance respecting divine things." A very basic but important spiritual principle to understand is that the accuser of the brethren has jurisdiction over the realm of darkness. When we operate in the dark, we are actually on the devil's playground. By operating in darkness, I mean functioning in ignorance, blindness, or even secrecy. The devil wants to keep us ignorant and spiritually blind; he wants to keep our true issues, battles, or struggles a secret because they can empower the demonic spirits that have been assigned to our lives.

Thus, the enemy doesn't want people to know the methods he is using and the schemes he is working against them. He doesn't want people to recognize the fortresses he is erecting in their minds, wills, and emotions because, when they are aware of them, his power can be broken. But knowledge is power!

In 2 Corinthians 10:5, the Bible commands us to "[cast] *down imagina-tions, and every high thing that exalts itself against the knowledge of God, and* [bring] *into captivity every thought to the obedience of Christ.*" When the light of the truth of God's Word illuminates our hearts and minds, the shifting shadows are dispersed.

A shadow is essentially the presence of some darkness. In contrast, the Scriptures tell us:

> *This then is the message which we have heard of Him, and declare to you, that God is light, and in Him is no darkness at all.* (1 John 1:5)

> *And the light shines in darkness; and the darkness comprehended it not.* (John 1:5)

The key to breaking the power of familiar spirits is to receive reve-lation from the Word of God regarding the area where there is oppres-sion or torment. For example, if you have thought that you are always the victim or that everyone is against you, and you finally come to the truth that you are a victor in Christ, those demonic thought patterns can be eliminated.

The enemy does not want us to expose to the light what he is doing. Millions of Christians all over the world are daily being bombarded by guilt, shame, and condemnation. The shame that they feel keeps them in cycles of defeat and bondage. There is an old adage, "Tell the truth and shame the devil!" This maxim is actually very scriptural. The Bible says:

> *Confess your faults one to another, and pray one for another, that you may be healed. The effectual fervent prayer of a righteous man avails much.* (James 5:16)

The apostle James admonishes us to confess our faults to one another. The Greek word translated *"confess"* is *exomologeō*, which can mean "to profess: acknowledge openly and joyfully." The Greek word for *"faults"* is *paraptōma*, which means "a lapse or deviation from truth and uprightness." The Bible is telling us to acknowledge where we have deviated from truth and uprightness. When we admit our sins to God (and before a spouse or another close family member or mature believer, when appropriate), we actually bring our shortcomings or struggles into the light, outside the jurisdiction of the accuser of the brethren. Remember, the devil can only operate in the darkness. Once we bring our sin or failure into the light through confession, the lying devil loses his power over us. It does not matter how embarrassing the sin is, you no longer need to fear being condemned. Why? The Bible tells us:

> *There is therefore now no condemnation to them which are in Christ Jesus, who walk not after the flesh, but after the Spirit.* (Romans 8:1)

One of the biggest lies that the enemy tells Christians is that if they confess their sins, people will judge them. This is an insidious tactic of the accuser to keep us in bondage. The truth is that people may judge or criticize you, but the greater truth is that you will be free. It is better to please God than to please men. This does not mean we should run around telling anyone and everyone our deepest, darkest secrets. But it does mean that we should be willing to humble ourselves and acknowledge when we were wrong about something.

ONCE WE BRING OUR SIN OR FAILURE INTO THE LIGHT THROUGH CONFESSION, THE LYING DEVIL LOSES HIS POWER OVER US.

Additionally, note that James 5:16 says, *"Confess your faults one to another, and pray one for another, **that you may be healed.**"* The Greek word rendered *"healed"* is *iaomai*, which means "to cure," "to heal," "to make whole: to free from errors and sins, to bring about (one's) salvation." When we confess our sins with a sincere heart of repentance and acknowledge our faults, we are made whole. Demons hate truth. Demons hate light. They hate accountability. If the enemy has been tormenting your life, bring your struggle before the light of God's countenance. Humble yourself before God, and His grace will deliver you. Hallelujah! Let's pray now!

PRAYER OF RELEASE

Father, I recognize, according to 1 Corinthians 2:16, that You have given me the mind of Christ; therefore, familiar spirits have no place influencing or negatively affecting my mind. I take authority over every demonic thought pattern or insidious paradigm that has given familiar spirits legal entry into my life. I cast down every imagination that is contrary to the Word of God, and I bring every thought captive to the obedience of Jesus Christ. In Jesus's name, I command oppression, depression, despair, and thoughts of rejection, worthlessness, hopelessness, and suicide to leave me, right now! All mental illness and its residue is driven out of my life. I am free! Thank You, Jesus!

INSIGHTS FOR OVERCOMING

1. The battlefield of spiritual warfare is in the mind.

2. Familiar spirits operate within the framework of people's thought patterns and paradigms. When a familiar spirit infests a person's paradigm, it becomes extremely difficult for that person to distinguish between their own thoughts and the thoughts planted by the enemy.

3. The goal of familiar spirits is not just to attack us physically or even spiritually but to cause us to embrace a mindset that is contrary to the Word of God.

4. To break the power of familiar spirits over our minds, we must receive revelation from the Word of God regarding the area where there is oppression or torment, acknowledge where we have deviated from truth and uprightness, and admit our sins to God (and before a spouse or another close family member or mature believer, when appropriate), with the assurance that there is no condemnation for those who are in Christ Jesus. We must reject false ideas and mindsets as soon as we recognize them in our lives.

PRACTICUM

1. Identify a negative thought pattern or paradigm (for example, perpetual feelings of condemnation or alienation) that you have been deceived by and need to let go of. Release this negative mindset to God and ask Him to replace the erroneous thoughts with His healing, freeing truths.

2. Building on the above exercise, write down several false and deceptive thoughts that you need to "cast down and take captive to the obedience of Christ," according to 2 Corinthians 10:4–5. Submit these thoughts to the truth of God's Word and daily remind yourself of the difference between what God says about them and what the enemy would say about them.

3. Make a decision to humbly acknowledge an area of sin or weakness to God and to a trusted friend or mentor. Bring this sin or weakness into the light of Christ so you can be made whole. If needed, seek additional counsel about the matter from a qualified Christian counselor.

13

EXPOSING HIDDEN ENEMIES

"And that because of false brethren unawares brought in, who came in secretly to spy out our liberty which we have in Christ Jesus, that they might bring us into bondage."
—Galatians 2:4

In chapter 12, we talked about how the enemy has jurisdiction over the realm of darkness. Darkness is the devil's playground. We discussed how familiar spirits love to hide behind the veil of our own thoughts and emotions. In this chapter, I want to further explore the dangerous dynamics of "hidden enemies" in our lives and how to recognize and expose them so that we can experience greater freedom in Christ.

I have always said that the most dangerous enemy is the one you do not see. David wrote,

Who can understand his errors? cleanse You me from secret faults. Keep back Your servant also from presumptuous ["deliberate" NLT] sins; let them not have dominion over me: then shall I be upright, and I shall be innocent from the great transgression. (Psalm 19:12–13)

David asked God to deliver him from *"secret faults."* The Hebrew word translated *"secret"* is *sātar,* which means "to hide" or "to conceal." In the context of this Scripture passage, it seems that the most dangerous enemy is within us—our hidden sins and iniquities. It is clear that the more hidden a sin or iniquity is, the greater danger it poses to our life and destiny. I believe that King David's plea for God to deliver him from hidden sin is a blueprint for spiritual warfare. God desires to expose every hidden enemy in our lives, whether internal or external. Hallelujah!

THE UNSEEN ADVERSARY

A friend of mine told me about a man who attended a conference where several famous preachers were speaking. This man was a retired law enforcement officer. During the time of altar ministry, he noticed a particular individual who walked to the front of the church to receive prayer from a well-known preacher. The retired officer could not take his eyes off the man who was being prayed for. Then, something came over the officer, and he ran and tackled the man receiving prayer. Everyone in the church was astonished. They screamed at him for tackling the innocent parishioner and shouted, "Get off of him!"

The church's security team scrambled to the scene and asked the former officer to please let the man get up off the ground. They told him it was not necessary to accost anyone because security was present. Reluctantly, the retired officer got up off the parishioner but proceeded to ask security to search the man. Even though there was no apparent need to search him, the security team agreed because the officer insisted. To their surprise, they found a serrated assault knife in his pocket, which he admitted he had intended to use to cut the throat of the pastor!

What would have happened if this former law enforcement officer had not discerned the threat and acted accordingly? That preacher might have been killed before his time. But the officer's years of service had given him the knowledge and experience to detect that something was wrong and to intervene.

Like the well-known pastor who didn't see the threat to his life, many Christians are suffering all sorts of afflictions and bondage in their spiritual lives because they are oblivious to the unseen enemy. They are unaware that this enemy poses a threat to their having a sustained spiritual walk and growing in God. The unseen adversary operates in *darkness*—in other words, in our ignorance. As we previously discussed, familiar spirits can function as "monitoring spirits" or informants, announcing to the enemy where there are open doors in our lives. It is necessary for these hidden enemies to be exposed so that we can remove them and walk in freedom. Like that retired law enforcement officer, we must learn to detect the "hidden enemy" and act according to the Word of God to secure our deliverance and healing.

THE DISCERNING OF SPIRITS

Previously, we discussed the importance of exercising the gift of discerning of spirits. Throughout the years of my life and ministry, my need for discernment has become more and more evident to me. In fact, on a number of occasions, spiritual discernment has literally saved my life, and I want to share with you what I have learned about this vital area. We will explore ways in which we can use this gift to detect, expose, and overcome hidden enemies.

Years ago, I did an exercise with my children to teach them about discernment. First, I brought out two clear plastic containers from the kitchen, and I proceeded to put sugar in one container and salt in the other. Then I asked my children to join me and tell me which container was filled with salt and which was filled with sugar. As you can imagine, they had a difficult time distinguishing between the two substances just by looking at them. They could tell the difference only after tasting them. I told them that there will be people and circumstances in their lives that might look one way but would actually be something totally different from what they seemed. I wanted them to understand that things are not always as they appear to be. My children were very receptive to this lesson.

To better understand what it means to exercise discernment, let's review Hebrews 5:14:

> But strong meat belongs to them that are of full age, even those who by reason of use have their senses exercised to discern both good and evil.

The Greek word translated "discern" is diakrisis, which means "a distinguishing, discerning, judging," as in knowing the difference between two things. The writer of Hebrews was essentially telling us that we must exercise the spiritual skill of distinguishing between good and evil. This a very important spiritual principle when it comes to overcoming familiar spirits because the differences between good and evil are not always immediately obvious.

The Bible says, "*Woe to them that call evil good, and good evil; that put darkness for light, and light for darkness; that put bitter for sweet, and sweet for bitter!*" (Isaiah 5:20). We are living in a time when spiritual and moral lines have become increasingly blurred. Unfortunately, our culture has become more and more deviant in these last days. The greatest form of deception is the belief that the things God calls profane are holy, and the things that God calls holy are profane.

Moreover, the danger is that the demonic realm is unseen to the natural eyes. Therefore, there are times when malevolent forces are operating and would be undetectable to those without a strong ability to discern good and evil. Sometimes, our "*presumptuous*" or "*willful*" (NLT) sins, as David called them in Psalm 19:12, are, unbeknownst to us, precipitated by demonic spirits. And sometimes our negative external circumstances are caused by these hidden enemies. We need to be able to discern such encroachments from the kingdom of darkness.

WE MUST EXERCISE THE SPIRITUAL SKILL OF DISTINGUISHING BETWEEN GOOD AND EVIL.

Several years ago, I went through the worst spiritual battle I had ever faced in my Christian life. What made it even harder was the fact that, while I was going through it, I did not know exactly whom to trust. Have you ever felt that way? I had given someone very close to me great access to my life, and the devil used this person to attack me further. As I confided in this person and shared the details of what I was going through, the situation became worse, and I could not understand what was happening. Months earlier, the Lord had shown me the true character of this individual, but I had refused to accept or heed His warnings.

One day, the Lord gave me a prophetic dream in which this person was sitting in a dark room. When I went to confront them about the things they were doing and saying, a knife came out of their mouth and traveled to the top of their head. In the dream, I felt a strong admonition from the Lord to refrain from engaging this person any further. When I woke up from the dream, I began to pray. The Lord told me that this individual had been using slander as a form of witchcraft. I knew that fighting them with my own reason and might were not going to yield results.

Instead, I went before the courts of heaven and asked God to issue an injunction against the lies and slander that were being spoken by this person. I took authority over the spirit of witchcraft operating in and through them, and, to my surprise, things began to turn around. I was delivered from that situation, and our ministry experienced a greater level of blessing and increase than we had seen to that point.

Many times, we do not recognize when familiar spirits are operating through people. But once the Lord exposes the unseen enemies, the efficacy of their attack can be significantly diminished or nullified. We must use our spiritual authority to shut down the devil and his clandestine schemes.

THE JUDAS SPIRIT

Let's look at another way unseen demonic spirits operate in people's lives. We all know the very prominent gospel accounts about Judas Iscariot, the disciple who betrayed Jesus. But there is something in his story that we can all learn from that I call the "Judas spirit." In fact, if we do not understand the nuances of the Judas spirit, we run the risk of being its next victim.

> *Then entered Satan into Judas surnamed Iscariot, being of the number of the twelve. And he went his way, and communed with the chief priests and captains, how he might betray Him to them.*
> (Luke 22:3–4)

The name Judas is a transliteration of the name Judah, which literally means "he shall be praised." Names are very important in the Bible, but they can reveal an even deeper reality about the spiritual realm, such as this: the Judas spirit is one of *false praise*. Some of the most diabolical attacks that I have undergone in my life were accompanied by false praise.

Counterfeit praise is a telling sign that the Judas spirit is in operation. The disciple Judas sat with Jesus, ate with Him, and even ministered with Him, yet his heart was fertile ground for betrayal and treachery. I don't believe Judas was an outwardly evil or sinister person, but I do think there was a spirit of greed and selfish ambition operating in his life that led to his destruction.

How can someone sing your praises one day and slander you the next? They are under the influence of a Judas spirit. One of the keys to dealing with this spirit is making sure that your own heart is pure. Jesus said, *"Hereafter I will not talk much with you: for the prince of this world comes, and has nothing in Me"* (John 14:30). What did He mean by the statement *"the prince of this world comes, and has nothing in Me"*? Jesus was saying that He had nothing in common with the prince of this world, who is the devil. There was no similarity or congruence between Him and the enemy. Therefore, there were no legal grounds by which the accuser could bring a legitimate accusation against Him.

I once went through a very difficult experience with betrayal. It was distressing because I had thought the person involved was my friend. They would often sing my praises, yet they were under the influence of a Judas spirit. One day, a pastor from Texas came and ministered to our congregation. He called me out of the crowd and gave me a profound word of knowledge, telling me that I was going through a difficult season and that there was a battle for my heart. He then proceeded to tell me that I was supposed to pray for the very person who had betrayed me. I was totally shocked at his words because he knew nothing about the situation I was going through at that time. I realized that I needed to obey this biblical command:

> *Be not overcome of evil, but overcome evil with good.*
>
> (Romans 12:21)

We must keep our hearts pure. We must walk in love and forgive freely. These are weapons against the Judas spirit that will dismantle its influence in our lives and ministries. It is important to remember that Jesus died on the cross to free us from *all* forms of wickedness, sin, and spiritual death. He also died for the betrayers in our lives and ministries. It is impossible for us to overcome the unseen familiar spirits operating in others without the discernment and leading of the Spirit. We must submit the Judas spirit to the fire of the Holy Spirit and ask the Lord for help in praying for those who are under the influence of that demonic spirit.

WE MUST KEEP OUR HEARTS PURE. WE MUST WALK IN LOVE AND FORGIVE FREELY.

THE DISSEMBLING SPIRIT

But when Peter was come to Antioch, I withstood him to the face, because he was to be blamed. For before that certain came from James, he did eat with the Gentiles: but when they were come, he withdrew and separated himself, fearing them which were of the circumcision. And the other Jews dissembled likewise with him; insomuch that Barnabas also was carried away with their dissimulation. (Galatians 2:11–13)

In the book of Galatians, the apostle Paul deals with the problem of legalism and its damaging effects on the early church. He rebukes the "Judaizers," or the adherents of legalistic behavior, for their hypocrisy and treatment of the Gentile believers. What does this account have to do with familiar spirits? Great question! There is an unseen spirit of artifice that is operating in the church today that has caused much frustration and pain. This spirit undermines relationships, sows strife and discord, and even bewitches unsuspecting believers into embracing a mindset that is antithetical to the gospel of Christ.

For many years, I faced setbacks and hindrances in ministry that I could not understand or explain. If you have ever served in ministry, you may be able to identify with what I am describing. For example, I can remember a specific instance where I had been invited to appear on a major Christian television network with another pastor. At the time, this was a mind-blowing opportunity for our ministry to receive the exposure it needed. However, when I contacted the producer to get the final details for the show, I never received a response. I called several times, to no avail. Later, I was watching this TV program when I saw the pastor whom I had been invited to appear with being interviewed. I could not understand why I had been left out, yet I had an eerily familiar feeling about it. At different times in my life, similar things had happened where I had been left out of something. I call the familiar spirit behind such occurrences "the dissembling spirit."

In Paul's description of his infamous meeting with the apostle Peter, he uses the word "*dissembled.*" The Greek word is *synypokrinomai,* which means "to act hypocritically with." "To dissemble" means "to hide under a false appearance" or "to put on the appearance of."[26] The aspect of this word that I want to focus on is the notion that there are people who act one way around a certain group of people but then act a different way around another group of people. I have seen instances where ministers will act like friends in one setting, but those same ministers will seek to undermine and sabotage each other's ministries in a different setting. This is not just a character issue with those particular leaders; there is a familiar spirit working in their lives. Sometimes people are oblivious to the fact that the dissembling spirit is operating in and through them. When I finally received a revelation of what this spirit is and how it operates, I began to take authority over it. Since that time, I have seen greater success in my life and ministry relationships.

REVISITING THE SPIRIT OF SABOTAGE

Earlier we talked about spirits of sabotage that rear their ugly heads by drawing people into wrong affiliations and connections that work to hinder their spiritual progress in God. The work of such spirits is often hidden. However, they will become easier to identify as we look to the light of the Word of God and the Spirit of Truth to reveal the true agendas of the people we interact with in life. Like people who are influenced by other types of familiar spirits, many who have been compromised by leaving an

---

26. *Merriam-Webster.com Dictionary,* s.v. "dissemble," https://www.merriam-webster.com/dictionary/dissemble.

open door to a spirit of sabotage are not aware that this spirit is functioning within them.

Beloved, we must not be passive toward the familiar spirits that are working to undermine our walk in Christ. There are unseen demonic forces that are manipulating or trying to manipulate us into relationships and experiences that are contrary to God's best for us. Again, spirits of sabotage work to deliberately destroy, damage, or obstruct God's plan and destiny for our lives.

We must understand this important spiritual principle: everything that takes place in the natural realm is precipitated by something in the spiritual realm. For example, if you seem to change friends once a year, it may be that unseen demonic forces are affecting your vital relationships. These spirits try to negatively influence people's attitudes toward you, and vice versa. Be mindful of the spiritual atmosphere that surrounds certain events or circumstances in your life. If you notice a pattern of unsettling events or the manifestation of an unhealthy type of person in your life during a particular period or time of year, then you may be dealing with a familiar spirit.

During one period of my life, I noticed that every year, around the same time, a certain type of disruptive person would come to our ministry. It was as if we were dealing with the same person from a previous season, only in a different body. At times, they would even possess the same attributes, personality, or mannerisms as the earlier person. Pay attention to occurrences such as this! Usually, the enemy will use such people or situations to keep you trapped in a cycle of confusion or confrontation. Begin to take authority over the spirit of sabotage operating in the person or circumstance. It does not matter how things appear; lean on the gift of discerning of spirits and ask God to expose what has been hidden. Once God has exposed the enemy, do not deny what you are seeing. Instead, break the cycle, in Jesus's name!

WE MUST NOT BE PASSIVE TOWARD THE FAMILIAR SPIRITS THAT ARE WORKING TO UNDERMINE OUR WALK IN CHRIST.

MARINE SPIRITS

As we grow in the gift of discerning of spirits, we can learn to sense the spiritual atmosphere around us and to recognize how familiar spirits are working their attacks in the physical world. In chapter 1, I described how principalities and demonic spirits are not omnipresent, and therefore they are assigned as "territorial spirits" to various countries, regions, states, cities, and communities. I also mentioned how, in my travels, I have found that particular countries or cities are under the influence of certain demonic strongholds. One type of territorial spirit is the "marine spirit."

As I wrote in my book *Kingdom Authority*, the first time I heard about marine spirits was when I was ministering in Liberia, West Africa, some years ago. One night, I was exhausted and recuperating after a long day of preaching and teaching, and I seemed to fall asleep and begin to dream. However, I realized I was not really having a dream; I had fallen into a trance and was seeing a vision, yet this vision was not from God. In the vision, I saw a young girl who was about seven or eight years old, and she was leading me down a pathway.

I thought it was strange that the young girl's face was identical to the face of a girl I had known in elementary school. Because her face was familiar, I trusted her, even though, in the vision, she hadn't grown to be an adult but was the same age as when I knew her. She led me to a building, and we went down a corridor and then through a door into a room. The girl said, "Follow me," so I followed her toward the bathroom. There, she transformed into a grown woman with a different face who had long hair that covered various parts of her body, but she was not clothed. Then she said, "Touch me," and as I stretched out my hands to touch her, I realized that this was a satanic apparition. I knew it was not from God but from the devil, and I began to take authority over that spirit.

I came out of the trance, and, in the process, I felt the most satanic, the most diabolical, the filthiest presence I had ever felt in my life. I immediately called my wife, and we began to pray over the phone. We racked up a nine-hundred-dollar international phone bill, but I needed to conduct spiritual warfare with the support of my wife.

The next day, my hosts were driving to the red-light district in Monrovia, and I saw the image of a woman on the side of a building. It was a picture of exactly the same woman I had seen in my dream! The Lord spoke to me and said, "This is the principality of this region." When I talked to the local pastor concerning this matter, I asked him what was going on. One reason I asked was that we had ministered to a number of young women, and most of them were unmarried, had given birth to children out of wedlock, were having all kinds of reproductive problems, had difficulty conceiving, or had suffered miscarriages. The pastor replied, "Marine spirits."

Some communities and traditions refer to marine spirits as "mermaids." In West Africa, the term is *mami wata*. In the Dominican Republic and other Latin-American Caribbean areas, marine spirits are referred to as *Yemaya* or the queen of the sea. Each of these cultures, as well as previous civilizations, has acknowledged that there is such a thing as a marine spirit, marine demon, or mermaid. These are demonic spirits that have an assignment to seduce, manipulate, and control but also to bind people or to bring people into slavery to the lust of the flesh.

On a different occasion, while I was preaching on the African continent, I had an encounter with a spirit that was operating through a particular person, and I became extremely sick. I had all the symptoms of cholera; I needed to use the restroom about twenty to thirty times in a matter of hours, and I was losing weight. It was truly a demonic attack. The Lord finally said to me, "How long are you going to take this?"

After the encounter with this spirit, I had begun to wrestle in my mind with the lust of the flesh. It was not about committing physical acts of sin but rather a struggle in my thoughts. I was tired, lethargic, and trying to battle through. At this time, one of my spiritual daughters gave me a call and said, "Apostle Kynan, I saw you in a dream, and in the dream you were lying on your bed. As you were lying on your bed, there were marines that were mermaids all around you, and they were whispering in your ear. They would then say to each other, 'He won't listen to us; we are trying everything we can, but he won't listen, he just won't listen.' They left you afterward because they could not capture you, but they tried. After they left you, they began to take pastors into captivity and bring them into the sea." After hearing about her dream, I understood what was going on in my situation; it was another attack from marine spirits.

This type of attack is real. Marine spirits are demons on a mission to pervert and destroy people by influencing them to give way to lust, seduction, and manipulation. It would be safe to say that behind every major fall, every major scandal, every major moral failure in the body of Christ, marine spirits and/or Jezebel spirits have been involved. Please understand that this is not a matter of scapegoating or making excuses for wrong behavior. We must be responsible for our own actions, we must be diligent, and we must walk in holiness, as Christ has called us to do. Yet most people are ignorant of the various unseen workings of the spiritual realm and the dangers of the kingdom of darkness. They must have their eyes opened and learn to engage in spiritual warfare if they are to defeat these familiar spirits.

> AS WE GROW IN THE GIFT OF DISCERNING OF SPIRITS,
> WE CAN LEARN TO SENSE THE SPIRITUAL ATMOSPHERE AROUND
> US AND TO RECOGNIZE HOW FAMILIAR SPIRITS ARE WORKING
> THEIR ATTACKS IN THE PHYSICAL WORLD.

I have seen marine spirits manifested all over the world. I have seen both the attacks and the negative consequences they bring. In the coastal areas of many countries or regions, there is a prevalence of perversion, immorality, and fornication. When you go to certain areas like Miami Beach or Daytona Beach in Florida, and to many islands in the Caribbean, there are festivals and ceremonies that are influenced by these marine spirits. Why? Because of the presence and manifestation of marine principalities. Marine spirits are the culprit behind children being molested, women being perverted at an early age, and men being seduced and perverted in their formative years. I receive so many prayer requests from happily married women who tell me, "I have sexual experiences in my sleep every day." These are *incubus* and *succubus* spirits. Many pastors and ministers do not talk about such encounters, but we can't afford to be ignorant about them; we need to be mindful of these divisive, demonic spirits so that we can combat them in the power of God.

One day, feeling under attack again in the area of sexual purity, and thinking it had solely to do with the fleshly nature, I prayed, "God, I need to be free. I need to get this off of me. I don't know what this is. I don't know why I'm struggling." I had gone to spiritual fathers, to leaders in the body of Christ, to receive counsel; I had written books on deliverance, including *Kingdom Authority*. I'd written books on the Jezebel spirit. So, I understood how these spirits operate, and yet I didn't realize what was happening at the time. As I prayed, the Lord explained to me, "Son, this is not just an issue with your flesh; you are dealing with marine spirits." After the Lord showed me what I had been dealing with, I literally felt the blanket of oppression lift from me. I cannot explain it. It just broke! God had done it supernaturally.

Marine spirits target spiritual leaders more than anyone else. In fact, spiritual leaders are their targets of choice. I heard a story in Nigeria about a woman who was stranded on the side of the road. A man who was driving by stopped to check on her, asking, "Hey, ma'am, do you need any help?" The woman replied, "Are you a pastor?" He said, "No, I'm not a pastor." She dismissed him, saying, "Go! I'm looking for pastors. I want pastors. I'm after pastors. If you are not a pastor, I don't want to talk to you."

The Scripture says,

My people are destroyed for lack of knowledge.   (Hosea 4:6)

People are destroyed for a lack of knowledge, and the devil exploits our blind spots. When we are ministering in countries or regions where marine spirits are prevalent, we need to understand the spiritual ramifications of what we are exposing ourselves to. We do not need to be fearful because we have spiritual authority in Christ. However, we ought to be vigilant and prepared for the warfare. Anytime you engage in a spiritual battle, you need to understand the territory and terrain you are going into. Beloved, we must be aware of the wiles of our enemy!

THE SPIRIT OF PREMATURE DEATH

Years ago, I was in Nigeria attending a large church meeting with thousands of people. The pastor began praying against the "spirit of premature death." That was the first time I had heard such terminology. I later realized that the spirit of premature death is very real, and it is even referenced in the Bible. Let's look at an example from the ministry of the apostle Paul:

> And upon the first day of the week, when the disciples came together to break bread, Paul preached to them, ready to depart on the morrow; and continued his speech until midnight. And there were many lights in the upper chamber, where they were gathered together. And there sat in a window a certain young man named Eutychus, being fallen into a deep sleep: and as Paul was long preaching, he sunk down with sleep, and fell down from the third loft, and was taken up dead. And Paul went down, and fell on him, and embracing him said, Trouble not yourselves; for his life is in him. When he therefore was come up again, and had broken bread, and eaten, and talked a long while, even till break of day, so he departed. And they brought the young man alive, and were not a little comforted. (Acts 20:7–12)

Many people think this is a story about a boy who *almost* died. Yet this is a story about a boy who actually died but was resurrected by the apostle Paul in the power of the Spirit. I believe that this boy experienced premature death. The Bible says that Paul fell upon him and said, "*Trouble not yourselves; for his life is in him.*" The last phrase can be literally translated, "His soul is still in him." In other words, even though his body was dead, it was not his time to die. His death was premature.

Just because a person perishes does not mean it was their time to die. The spirit of premature death is behind suicide and many sudden and unexpected deaths. There are countless cases of people who were in perfect physical health falling dead for no apparent reason. The devil is a thief and a murderer. We must take authority over the spirit of premature death in the name of Jesus. Proclaim this verse over yourself and over your household:

> I shall not die, but live, and declare the works of the LORD.
> (Psalm 118:17)

DISCERNING AND CONFRONTING UNSEEN ENEMIES

In this chapter, we have looked at ways we can discern and expose hidden demonic enemies. In various aspects of our lives, we may not just be dealing with natural circumstances or people but with unseen spiritual forces that seek to impede the work of God in us and distract us from our heavenly assignments. However, once we understand this spiritual reality and then discern and confront any unseen enemies, we can walk in freedom and victory. Glory to God!

PRAYER OF RELEASE

Father God, Jeremiah 29:11 says that Your thoughts toward me are of peace and not of evil, and that You have an expected end for me. I ask the Holy Spirit to guide me in the discerning of spirits. I ask You, Father, to expose the enemy's hidden plans that have come against Your plan and destiny for my life. Forgive me for the times when I have knowingly or unknowingly operated according to a dissembling spirit, a Judas spirit, or any other hidden familiar spirit. I rebuke any spirits of sabotage operating in my relationships and spheres of influence. Father, grant me a pure heart. Remove from me anything that does not reflect Your character. I declare that Satan has no legitimate accusation against me because You are "for" me. I declare that, according to Psalm 68:1, the enemies of God in my life are scattered. I cancel every demonic assignment, every plot sent my way to destroy, damage, obstruct, hinder, or sabotage my spiritual calling. I come into agreement with Psalm 139:5, which says, *"You have beset me behind and before, and laid Your hand upon me."* Therefore, I am fully protected from any and every hidden enemy, in Jesus's mighty name. Amen!

INSIGHTS FOR OVERCOMING

1. God desires to expose every hidden enemy in our lives, whether internal or external.

2. The spiritual skill of distinguishing between good and evil is very important for overcoming familiar spirits because the differences between good and evil are not always immediately obvious. We are living in a time when spiritual and moral lines have become increasingly blurred. Moreover, the danger is that the demonic realm is unseen to the natural eyes.

3. Some hidden spiritual enemies are: the Judas spirit, the dissembling spirit, the spirit of sabotage, marine spirits, and the spirit of premature death.

4. In various aspects of our lives, we may not just be dealing with natural circumstances or people but with unseen spiritual forces that seek to impede the work of God in us and distract us from our heavenly assignments. However, once we understand this spiritual reality and then discern and confront any unseen enemies, we can walk in freedom and victory.

ASK YOURSELF

1. Have you been frustrated by recurring problems with circumstances and/or people? If so, will you ask God to show you if hidden enemy forces are playing a role in these situations and to enable you to discern what they are so you can overcome them?

2. Do you recognize any areas in your life where you may have allowed a familiar spirit to influence you to act in way that is dissembling or hypocritical toward others? If so, how will you respond in the future?

3. Have you been distracted from your heavenly assignment by other people or circumstances? How can you realign your life with God's purposes?

14

WALKING IN TOTAL FREEDOM

"If the Son therefore shall make you free, you shall be free indeed."
—John 8:36

I wrote this book to help Christians recognize and overcome the insidious familiar spirits that attack them daily, robbing them of their peace and victory. It is my earnest desire to see the body of Christ walking in total freedom and experiencing the abundant life in its completeness. This means that after we overcome familiar spirits, we need to *maintain* the freedom Christ has won for us.

The apostle Paul admonished the churches in Galatia, *"Stand fast therefore in the liberty wherewith Christ has made us free, and be not entangled again with the yoke of bondage"* (Galatians 5:1). He made this statement in the spiritual climate of the "Judaizers," the zealous religious believers we talked about in the previous chapter who advocated for legalism instead of grace and brought Gentile believers under bondage to the law.

Like the first-century church, we are commanded to stand fast in the freedom that Christ won for us in His death and resurrection and to not be *"entangled again with the yoke of bondage."* The Greek word translated *"entangled"* is *enechō*, among whose meanings are "to have within," "to hold in," or "to be held ensnared." Essentially, the Bible is telling us to not become ensnared by the bondage from which we have just been delivered.

How many times have you heard Christians refer to their *"thorn in the flesh"* (2 Corinthians 12:7) in reference to a sin, sickness, or affliction they are unable to overcome? In previous books and teachings, I have extensively expounded on what Paul was referring to by his "thorn of the flesh," so I will refrain from a detailed explanation in this book. However, I want to assure you that God's will is for you to walk in total freedom. The Scriptures are very clear about this: *"If the Son therefore shall make you free, you shall be free indeed"* (John 8:36).

We will return to this verse later in the chapter, but for now, I want to focus particular attention on the word *"indeed."* It is translated from the Greek word *ontōs*, which means "truly, in reality, in point of fact, as [opposed] to what is pretended, fictitious, false [or] conjectural." In other words, Jesus does not make us free in the sense of pretending that everything is okay when we are around other Christians but, in reality, remaining in bondage. He grants us true and lasting freedom. He changes our reality from that of captivity to that of liberty.

WE ARE COMMANDED TO STAND FAST IN THE FREEDOM THAT CHRIST WON FOR US IN HIS DEATH AND RESURRECTION AND TO NOT BE "ENTANGLED AGAIN WITH THE YOKE OF BONDAGE."

TWO DIFFERENT FOUNDATIONS

To maintain that liberty, we need a solid foundation. As a Florida resident, I have seen my share of storms. In fact, one of the worst hurricanes to hit our coast in years came right to my backyard. I remember it like it was yesterday! God miraculously delivered my family and me from that storm. (I talk about this incident in detail in my book *Invading the Heavens*.) Nonetheless, through that experience, I learned that, spiritually speaking, storms do not come to destroy us but to reveal our trust in God. If we are going to walk in total freedom as new covenant believers, we must learn to weather the storms that try our faith.

One of my favorite stories in the Gospels is Jesus's parable about the two houses in Matthew 7:24-27:

Therefore whosoever hears these sayings of Mine, and does them, I will liken him to a wise man, which built his house upon a rock: and the rain descended, and the floods came, and the winds blew, and beat upon that house; and it fell not: for it was founded upon a rock. And every one that hears these sayings of Mine, and does them not, shall be likened to a foolish man, which built his house upon the sand: and the rain descended, and the floods came, and the winds blew, and beat upon that house; and it fell: and great was the fall of it.

(Matthew 7:24–27)

Jesus said that whoever hears His words and does them is like a man who builds his house on a rock. When the storm comes and beats upon that house, the house remains standing. In contrast, whoever hears Jesus's words but refuses or neglects to obey them is like a foolish man who builds his house on sand. When the inevitable storm comes, that house cannot withstand the devastation and ultimately is destroyed.

It is very important to understand that in both scenarios, there was a storm. The difference was the foundation. According to Jesus, our reliance on Him and our obedience to the Word of God determines the type of foundation we build on, and ultimately whether or not our spiritual house will remain standing. Too many believers are building "sandcastles." No matter how beautiful a sandcastle may be, it will never withstand a flood. What foundation are you building upon? Obedience to Jesus is absolutely necessary for sustaining our deliverance from familiar spirits. Once we receive deliverance, we must maintain that deliverance through spiritual discipline. As we will shortly discuss, this includes the essential discipline of reading, hearing, meditating upon, and obeying God's Word.

DELIVERANCE PLUS DETERMINATION PLUS DISCIPLESHIP

Throughout my walk with the Lord, I have discovered that, many times, the enemy tries to convince us that we are not as "delivered" as we think we are. In previous chapters, I have talked about how there are times when we say, "I thought I was delivered from that!" only to find ourselves succumbing to that particular temptation once again. How can we move past this? We need to combine deliverance with determination (a commitment to maintaining our freedom) and discipleship.

As I indicated previously, years ago, I struggled with pornography. I remember telling my youth pastor that I was having a very hard time in this particular area. I even went to a men's conference and confessed my sin before the entire group of men because I was desperate for freedom. Here I was, born again and Spirit-filled, yet struggling with lust. I was so ashamed.

Unfortunately, many men at that conference were struggling with the same issue, and the only advice I was given was to "take it one day at a time." I thought to myself, "I don't want to take it one day at a time; I want to be completely free, right now!" I walked away from that conference very disappointed.

One day, while I was crying out to God for deliverance, I heard the Lord speak to me as clear as day: "Kynan, I already delivered you from this!" I was so perplexed by that statement that I enquired further. He told me, "You are choosing this!" Then, I got the revelation. There was deliverance in my *decision*. It took some time, but one day, in the middle of a worship service, I told the Lord, "I don't want this anymore. Take it from me! I choose You!" Instantly, I felt a weight lift off of me. I did not cough or spit up. I simply felt a release. After that, I even tried to go back and watch pornography, but I could not. Hallelujah! As I daily walked out that supernatural encounter, I experienced real and lasting freedom.

I am very thankful for the supernatural grace of God that delivered me from the power of addiction. However, as I expressed earlier, I honor that grace daily by choosing to turn my eyes from evil things. Please make no mistake: this is only possible by the grace of God, not by human strength or ability. The point is that there is something distinctively divine about making a quality decision to receive all that was provided for us by Jesus on the cross.

Let's look at this profound statement by Jesus:

Then said Jesus to those Jews which believed on Him, If you continue in My word, then are you My disciples indeed; and you shall know the truth, and the truth shall make you free. (John 8:31–32)

Many people quote John 8:32 out of context, neglecting to also quote verse 31. Jesus said explicitly, *"If you continue in My word, then are you My disciples indeed."* This is an "if-then" statement. It tells us that continuity in the Word of God produces discipleship. Jesus then said, *"And you shall know the truth, and the truth shall make you free."* These two verses are connected by the Greek conjunction *kai*, which means that the two ideas were conjoined by the writer of the text.

CONTINUITY IN THE WORD OF GOD PRODUCES DISCIPLESHIP.

Truly, maintaining our freedom requires both determination and discipleship. As I wrote earlier in this book, in today's church, we live in an age of "hyper-grace." Many well-intentioned preachers are presenting a truncated version of the Scriptures, giving people only part of the truth. As a result, many impressionable Christians equate the message of God's grace with a form of spiritual laziness that does not require any sacrifice or discipline because, after all, "Jesus paid it all!" While it is very true that Jesus paid it all, we must intentionally and consistently appropriate His finished work in every area of our lives. The apostle Paul puts it this way:

> *Wherefore, my beloved, as you have always obeyed, not as in my presence only, but now much more in my absence, work out your own salvation with fear and trembling.* (Philippians 2:12)

The Greek word rendered salvation is *sōtēria*, which literally means "deliverance." Paul tells the Philippian church to *"work out"* their deliverance with reverential fear. The words *"work out"* are translated from a compound Greek word, *katergazomai*. The prefix *kata* can signify "throughout," and the suffix *ergazomai* can mean "to labor" or "to exercise." A good analogy to describe the meaning of this word is that of a pastry chef kneading dough. They have to work from the inside out. The dough has everything it needs on the inside, but the pastry chef must "work it out" to see the full manifestation of the dough's potential.

Many people believe that if they go through the nearest "healing line" or set up an appointment with the best deliverance minister in town, then God will tap them with His magic wand and, voila! they will experience "freedom." Friends, it does not work that way! Does God deliver people instantly? Absolutely! We have many examples in Scripture where people received a miraculous touch from God. However, we have a responsibility to walk out our freedom daily.

ALTHOUGH JESUS "PAID IT ALL," WE MUST INTENTIONALLY AND CONSISTENTLY APPROPRIATE HIS FINISHED WORK IN EVERY AREA OF OUR LIVES.

MIND RENEWAL AS MIRACLE MAINTENANCE

There are many ways in which we walk out our freedom, such as regularly reading the Word of God, fellowshipping with other believers, praying, fasting, praising and worshipping the Lord, serving others, and giving to God's work. However, in this chapter, I want to focus on one significant way that we can maintain our freedom: renewing our minds. To keep from reverting to our old ways, we must change the way that we think! Romans 12:2 is very clear about this truth:

And be not conformed to this world: but be you transformed by the renewing of your mind, that you may prove what is that good, and acceptable, and perfect, will of God.

I love the word *"transformed"* in this passage. It comes from the Greek word *metamorphoō*, which literally means "to change into another form" or "to transfigure." It means to undergo a metamorphosis. We are called by God into a transformational experience through the *"renewing"* of our minds. The Greek word translated *"renewing"* is *anakainōsis*, which signifies "a renewal, renovation, complete change for the better."

As we change the way we think, it causes a renovation within us, which produces a transformation. Think of it this way: the renovation is the *process*, and the transformation is the *end result*. It is much like having your home renovated. When the contractors come in, they begin to demolish the old structures in order to build new structures. This demolition and construction is a process, but when it is complete, your house looks and feels brand new. Your home is literally transformed! *"Old things are passed away; behold, all things are become new"* (2 Corinthians 5:17).

Thus, when the Bible talks about deliverance, it is speaking about an all-encompassing reality. Romans 10:13 says, *"For whosoever shall call upon the name of the Lord shall be saved."* The apostle Paul was quoting Joel 2:32, *"And it shall come to pass, that whosoever shall call on the name of the LORD shall be **delivered**."* The Greek word translated *"saved"* in Romans 10:13 is *sozo*, which signifies "saved," "healed," "delivered," and "restored."

Suppose a firefighter rescued a woman from a burning building, but her body had been burned by the fire. If the firefighter were to merely leave her outside the building, lying on the ground, she would have been saved from the fire, but she would still be at risk because of the burns she sustained. He would need to bring her to an ambulance, which would take her to a hospital where there was a burn unit. The doctor would then need to treat the burns and prescribe medicine and possible therapy to ensure that the woman was restored to health. In the same way, God didn't just snatch us out of the fires of hell to leave us burned on the side of the road. He wants us to have joy, peace, and abundance. We can receive these things fully by the renewing of our minds, *"that [we] may prove what is that good, and acceptable, and perfect, will of God"* (Romans 12:2).

Everything I have shared about familiar spirits in this book boils down to this simple truth: God wants you to live the abundant life that He paid a heavy price to provide for you. Once you take authority over these demonic powers, confronting and renouncing them, you must build godly structures in your thinking that will facilitate and maintain a victorious life.

The enemy wants to tear us down, but God wants to build us up.

The enemy wants us to be isolated, but God draws us to Himself in love.

The enemy binds us in his lies, but God frees us in His truth.

Remain in God and His Word, *"and you shall know the truth, and the truth shall make you free"*—from familiar spirits and all the work of the enemy. Praise God!

INSIGHTS FOR OVERCOMING

1. We are commanded to stand fast in the freedom that Christ won for us in His death and resurrection and to not be *"entangled again with the yoke of bondage."*

2. Once we receive deliverance, we must maintain that deliverance through spiritual discipline.

3. Although Jesus "paid it all," we must intentionally and consistently appropriate His finished work in every area of our lives.

4. To keep from reverting to our old ways, we must change the way we think by renewing our minds with God's Word.

ABOUT THE AUTHOR

Dr. Kynan T. Bridges is the senior pastor of Grace & Peace Global Fellowship in Tampa, Florida. With a profound revelation of the Word of God and a dynamic teaching ministry, Dr. Bridges has revolutionized the lives of many in the body of Christ. Through his practical approach to applying the deep truths of the Word of God, he reveals the authority and identity of the new covenant believer.

God has placed on Dr. Bridges a particular anointing for understanding and teaching the Scriptures, along with the gifts of prophecy and healing. Dr. Bridges and his wife, Gloria, through an apostolic anointing, are committed to equipping the body of Christ to live in the supernatural every day and to fulfill the Great Commission. It is Dr. Bridges's desire to see the nations transformed by the unconditional love of God.

A highly sought speaker and published author of a number of books, his previous books with Whitaker House include *Unlocking the Code of the Supernatural, School of the Miraculous, Invading the Heavens, Unmasking the Accuser, The Power of Prophetic Prayer,* and *Kingdom Authority.* Dr. Bridges is a committed husband, a mentor, and a father of five beautiful children: Ella, Naomi, Isaac, Israel, and Anna.

Welcome to Our House!

We Have a Special Gift for You

It is our privilege and pleasure to share in your love of Christian books. We are committed to bringing you authors and books that feed, challenge, and enrich your faith.

To show our appreciation, we invite you to sign up to receive a specially selected **Reader Appreciation Gift**, with our compliments. Just go to the Web address at the bottom of this page.

God bless you as you seek a deeper walk with Him!

WE HAVE A GIFT FOR YOU. VISIT:

whpub.me/nonfictionthx

WHITAKER
HOUSE